HISTORIC
Mission Inn

GLENWOOD

ENTRE ES SU CASA AMIGO

CALIFORNIA'S
MISSION INN
RIVERSIDE.

RIVERSIDE, CALIFORNIA

PUBLISHED BY:

Friends of the Mission Inn
3668 Main St
Riverside, CA 92501
P.O. Box 1546
Riverside, CA 92502-1546
Phone: (909) 788-8090

EDITOR:

Barbara Moore

COORDINATOR:

Elaine Ford

ART DIRECTOR:

Robert Reed, RB Graphics

DESIGNER:

Jennifer Disbrow, RB Graphics

WRITERS:

Allene Archibald, Alan Curl, Joan Hall, Kevin Hallaran, Philippa Jones, Walter Parks, Michael Rounds, and Juanita Thinnes.

PHOTOGRAPHERS:

Michael J. Elderman, Robert Fitch, Judith Giberson, John Kleinman, Cean Oricotti, Bill Rose, Bill Roth, and Robert Torrez.

First Edition.
ISBN #0-9666914-0-7

Printed in Riverside, California by RB Graphics.

Jacket Photographs:

Front: The Amistad Dome with snow-covered San Bernardino Mountains in the background.

Back: Main entrance to the Mission Inn glittering with Christmas lights.

Other Photographs:

First end paper: Panoramic view of the Mission Inn in the 1930s.

Second end paper: Dated 1274 AD, the oldest known Christian bell hangs at the Mission Inn.

Page 1: The Mission Inn escutcheon offers a hospitable welcome to visitors.

Friends of the Mission Inn

Page 3: Flags flying on the Mission Inn entrance arch frame a view of the campanario and carillon.

Page 4 and 5: A 1910 tinted postcard showing Mission Inn guests setting off for a day of sightseeing.

Page 6: ST. FRANCIS OF ASSISI—a painting by George Melville Stone.

Page 7: The distinctive Rain Cross logo of the Mission Inn combines a double armed cross, found in many Indian cultures, with a suspended early California Mission style bell.

First book end paper: The Miller family transplants a navel orange tree in the Spanish Patio.

Second back end paper: The Mission Wing in 1909.

The River of Life design was a feature carved into many of the doors of the early California Missions. Symbolizing life with no beginning and no end, it has been a motif found on Mission Inn doors, panels and other woodwork since 1902.

CONTENTS

Preface ... 7

Welcome ... 9

In the Beginning –
Frank A. Miller ... 10

A Walk Around the Block ... 20

Court of the Birds ... 28

Ground Floor ... 36

First Floor ... 66

Upper Floors ... 96

Mission Inn Museum ... 110

Restoration and Renewal ... 116

Through the Years ... 122

Acknowledgements ... 124

Photo Credits ... 125

Index ... 127

PREFACE

Since the Mission Inn's Grand Opening Gala in 1993, there have been numerous requests for a new publication highlighting the rejuvenation of this National Landmark hotel. The Friends of the Mission Inn voted to undertake the challenging project and provided the funds to make it possible.

The Friends of the Mission Inn was founded by Patsy O'Toole in 1969 to help prevent the financially strapped hotel from closing its doors or—even worse—from being demolished. The members of this volunteer group not only have donated money but have given freely of their time and services. The organization is committed to the preservation of the historic collections of furniture, art, and artifacts gathered by the Miller family.

Moneys for these projects come from membership dues, fund raisers, and proceeds from the Inn-Credible Gift Corner. Hundreds of thousands of dollars have been spent on repairing and restoring many valuable art objects in the Mission Inn's fine collections.

Writers, photographers, and curators—enthusiastic volunteers all—have collaborated to tell the story of this wonderful hotel. The end result is an armchair tour through the Mission Inn, interlaced with a bit of history and an anecdote or two.

Jolyn Jensen, *President*
Friends of the Mission Inn

Mission Inn owner Duane Roberts and his family.

WELCOME

$\mathcal{I}$ was honored when the Friends of the Mission Inn asked me to write the "Welcome" for this important artistic creation. I was also grateful, for it presented me with the opportunity to thank all those who have given so much time, effort, and unyielding commitment to ensuring that the Mission Inn would survive and flourish through the years.

And flourish it has! Having been restored to its original grandeur, the hotel is once again the heart of the region and unmistakably one of the grand hotels of America. Just as important, the Mission Inn is the architectural centerpiece of our wonderful city of Riverside. It is a meeting place for friends and family, a place to dine in architectural splendor, and a place to wed and begin lives together.

And yet none of this would be possible without the past and continued support of significant community organizations. The Friends of the Mission Inn is to be highly commended for its stalwart support throughout the years, including its expert restoration of important Mission Inn artwork and for creating this lasting tribute to the extraordinary history of this grand property. The Mission Inn Foundation must be thanked for adding to the unparalleled ambiance of the Mission Inn by allowing much of its artwork to be displayed in the hotel and for operating the extraordinarily educational Mission Inn Museum. And I wish to express my sincere gratitude to the Mission Inn Foundation Docents, our great ambassadors, who continue to share with the world the fascinating story of the Mission Inn.

Finally, I would be remiss if I didn't extend my gratitude to the two groups of individuals who are the true lifeblood of this great hotel: our guests and our employees. The Mission Inn is a place where guests come to escape to another world, to relax, and to appreciate the historic significance of this hotel. Without them, the doors of this great place could not remain open. And to our wonderful employees: thank you for your commitment to providing the highest quality of hospitality in the industry—the reason so many guests return time and time again.

When I was a boy growing up in Riverside, I would visit the Mission Inn, occasionally sneaking into areas off limits to guests such as the mysterious Catacombs underneath the hotel. I was captivated by the history, the architecture, the wonder of the hotel. Little did I know then that someday I would have the privilege of owning and operating this historic treasure. The friendships I have made through the hotel and the memories the hotel has created for others, have enriched my life. On behalf of the entire Mission Inn family, I look forward to many years of continued friendships and meaningful memories.

Duane R. Roberts
"Keeper of the Inn"

IN THE BEGINNING...

FRANK AUGUSTUS MILLER
Master of the Inn
1857–1935

When 17-year-old Frank Miller first set eyes on Riverside, California, he wrote glumly in his diary that the town was a "desiloate plain." The next few years, however, would bring two major changes. First, his spelling would improve under the influence of his wife, Isabella Hardenburg, Riverside's first woman school teacher, whom he married in 1880. Second, a boom in the citrus industry would transform Riverside into one of the most luxuriant landscapes in the United States.

Oval: Young Frank Miller
Large picture: An early Riverside citrus grove.

Riverside was founded in 1870 as a planned agricultural colony for Easterners who wanted to spend their winters in a warmer climate. The citrus industry began almost accidentally in 1873 with the arrival of two Brazilian navel orange trees, shipped to Eliza and Luther Tibbets from the Department of Agriculture in Washington, DC. By 1885 Riverside orange growers would capture the gold and silver medals of the New Orleans World's Industrial and Cotton Centennial Exposition and begin proclaiming Riverside as the "Greatest Orange Growing City in the World." Just a decade later Riverside was the wealthiest city per capita in the nation.

Canals were the lifeblood of this fledgling desert community. In 1874 Frank Miller's father, Christopher Columbus Miller, was commissioned to expand the existing canal system of the Riverside Colony Association. A civil engineer who had served in the Union Army during the Civil War, C. C. Miller moved from Wisconsin to California after his wife's doctor advised a change of climate for her health.

The cash-poor Colony Association paid C. C. Miller with its main asset—land. In 1875 C. C. Miller took possession of a full block on Main Street in what would become downtown Riverside. That same year the town's first brick store was built among a sprinkling of small wooden and adobe buildings.

Christopher Columbus Miller and his wife, Mary.

Guests arrived at the Glenwood by stagecoach in the 1890s.

A year later the Millers built their house. They used the cheapest building material available, adobe bricks made of mud and straw, but covered the structure with clapboard siding to look more "Eastern" and thus, respectable. Frank, the older son of the four Miller children, worked alongside Indian laborers, recalling it later as some of the most back-breaking drudgery he had ever done. To save on rent, the family moved in before the roof was finished or the windows installed. By November the house had a name—Glenwood Cot-

Mild Riverside winters enticed Easterners to stay at the Glenwood.

tage—and the Millers began taking in paying guests as a source of income. The first was Albert S. White, a wealthy New Yorker, who came to spend the winters and ended up as a permanent resident of both Riverside and the Miller family hotel.

Nineteen-year-old Miller worked himself into exhaustion on a series of odd jobs, building up capital for his future endeavors. Soon he had an orange grove and a downtown grocery store, where he discovered his gift for promotion and sales, a skill that would serve him well in the following years. While Frank was establishing himself, the other family members were building Glenwood Cottage into a small hotel.

In 1880 Frank bought the hotel and its entire block from his father and two years later added another wing, nearly doubling the size. His sister Alice, who served as manager, was responsible for

Frank Miller and his wife Isabella enjoy a quiet moment.

The new Glenwood Mission Inn in 1903.

the Glenwood's growing reputation for hospitality and homelike atmosphere.

Inland Southern California was not only a center of citrus horticulture but a resort region as well. The dry warmth and the scent of blossoms attracted winter-bound tourists who tended to spend months in one place, and resort hotels became an important factor in economic growth. As the visitors relaxed, many looked for investment opportunities or permanent homes. Miller saw millionaires flocking to hotels in Pasadena and Redlands, while Riverside attracted the second tier of wealthy travelers. It was time to build a modern hotel with all the latest comforts to entice more prosperous guests.

After a decade of trying to lure investors to the new hotel, Miller finally found a backer in railroad magnate, Henry E. Huntington. Today we can be grateful for those years of delay, for Miller's blueprints of the 1890s called for an ordinary hotel. While he negotiated for funds and waited for financing, Miller drew plan after plan. In all

variations, he kept the central gardens, a west wing for shops, and the common U-shape of the building, later adding towers and other design elements.

Around the turn of the century, Los Angeles architect Arthur Burnett Benton became an advocate for the Mission Revival architectural style in Southern California. This romantic inspiration from California's Spanish Colonial heritage

Naturalists John Muir and John Burroughs in the garden of the Mission Inn in 1907.

appealed to Miller and, not surprisingly, Benton was his architect of choice. When construction began on the new structure in 1902, the seeds had been sown for a hotel like no other in the world.

Miller cleared the site by moving some of the Glenwood buildings to the back of the block and demolishing others. Never sentimental about his own past, he planned to tear down the original adobe cottage he had helped build. His daughter Allis, who had been born in the cottage in 1882, pleaded for its retention, so Miller remodeled his family home into a classic Spanish adobe and called it the Old Adobe.

When the new hotel opened as the Glenwood Mission Inn in 1903, Miller knew he had his grand hotel, but only with the public response did he realize he had created a legend. Falling under the spell of the place as surely as did any visitor, Miller added to his legend, bit by bit over the next thirty years. The skilled promoter wanted one thing for his hotel—more.

Miller and his family traveled the world, shipping back tons of artifacts, and the hotel grew to accommodate them all. Even though Riverside had never been the site of a Franciscan mission,

Arthur B. Benton's 1902 architectural drawing for the new Glenwood Mission Inn.

> *"The comfort and hospitality of a simple home, luxury and service of a palace all combined in the Glenwood Mission Inn."*
>
> SUNSET MAGAZINE
> *December 1909*

Frank A. Miller, Master of the Inn.

the Glenwood Mission Inn gradually became famous as the Mission Inn, a museum as well as a hotel. Miller also attracted great people of the day, who left their names and their ideas behind in the giant mosaic of the Inn, where the future took shape from the past.

Frank Augustus Miller's life exemplified his beliefs. He was a humanist, a prohibitionist, and a tireless worker for international peace. The Mission Inn is Frank Miller's autobiography and that of his family. Every idea they had, every place they went, every joy they felt, left their marks on this building. Probably no other hotel in the United States can claim to have had the same proprietor for over 55 years. The hotel remained the center of Frank Miller's life until he died in 1935.

Here is the extraordinary story the Mission Inn tells.

In 1914, Frank Miller and his guest Booker T. Washington share the panoramic view of Riverside from Mount Rubidoux.

Frank Miller at the entrance of the Glenwood Mission Inn.

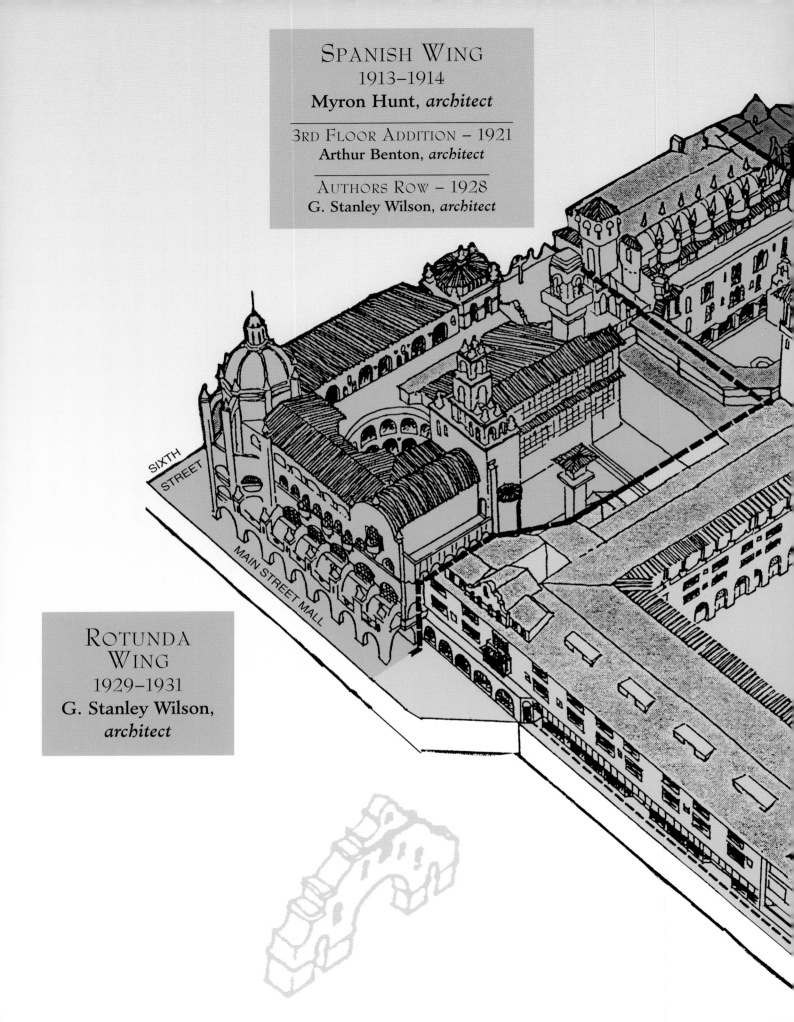

SPANISH WING
1913–1914
Myron Hunt, *architect*

3RD FLOOR ADDITION – 1921
Arthur Benton, *architect*

AUTHORS ROW – 1928
G. Stanley Wilson, *architect*

ROTUNDA
WING
1929–1931
G. Stanley Wilson,
architect

SIXTH
STREET

MAIN STREET MALL

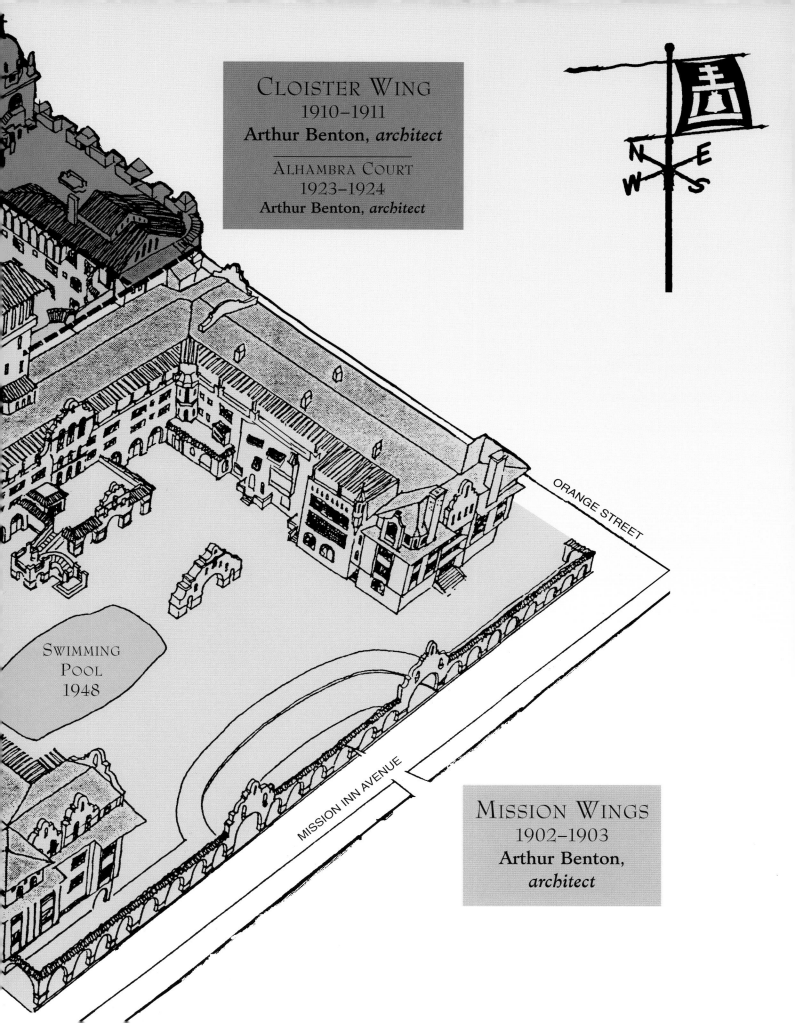

CLOISTER WING
1910–1911
Arthur Benton, *architect*

ALHAMBRA COURT
1923–1924
Arthur Benton, *architect*

ORANGE STREET

SWIMMING
POOL
1948

MISSION INN AVENUE

MISSION WINGS
1902–1903
Arthur Benton,
architect

N E S W

A WALK AROUND THE BLOCK

The rambling Mission Inn fills more than an entire city block, covering two and one-half acres. Varying in height from four to six stories, with half-hidden steps and narrow, winding stairways, the interior of the Mission Inn is a maze of courtyards, terraces, balconies, and patios. The Inn's geography can be perplexing as it moves from one building style to another; a tour of the exterior helps identify the principal parts.

Massive stucco arches topped with red roof tiles line Mission Inn Avenue and mark the main entrance to the Mission Inn. The arches were built in 1908 to resemble the arcades of both the Mission San Juan Capistrano and Mission San Luis Rey, and for many years were known as the Seventh Street Arches. Although the name of the street has been changed

Mission style arches along Mission Inn Avenue mark the main entrance to the Mission Inn.

Rain Cross light standards line Orange Street with Carmel Tower Dome in the background.

to Mission Inn Avenue, the arches continue to identify the historic Mission Inn. During the 1985 restoration, the arches were replaced with exact replicas because the originals did not meet modern seismic codes.

Near the main entrance on Mission Inn Avenue, a rough brick wall laced with wrought iron grating extends along the sidewalk toward Orange Street. Embedded in the low wall of bricks are several weathered crests and carved stone heads from pre-Aztec deities.

At the corner of Orange Street and Mission Inn Avenue, an angled wrought iron grille gate provides privacy for the landscaped garden and

Decorative brick walls border the Mission Inn Avenue sidewalk.

the four stories of guest rooms that rise above it. This is part of the Mission Wing, the oldest section of the hotel, designed by architect Arthur B. Benton and built in 1902.

Facing Orange Street are several different styles of doors that lead to private suites. These suites also have doors that open into the Court of the Birds. A blue canopy extending over the Orange Street entrance to the hotel lobby marks the end of the Mission Wing and the beginning of the Cloister Wing, with its distinctive round bay of leaded glass windows.

Also designed by Benton and borrowing freely from various California Missions, the Cloister Wing was built in 1910. Arching over the sidewalk are four one-story flying buttresses. Hotel rooms with stained glass windows and small balconies complete the Cloister Wing. Near the corner of Orange and Sixth Streets is a decorative frame doorway, a copy of the entrance to the Carmel Mission. On the roof above is a replica of the Carmel Mission tower, a large red dome that has become a Riverside landmark, overlooking Orange Street and the street lights patterned after the Inn's logo, the Rain Cross.

Past the Carmel Mission facade, a change of architecture occurs again on Sixth Street with the beginning of the Spanish Wing, which was designed by Myron Hunt and completed in 1915. Decorative high-arched windows in the massive walls of poured concrete mark the location of the two-story Spanish Art Gallery. On the upper tier of this section are the impressive hotel

Weathered crests are embedded in the brick walls.

The Mission Wing extends along Orange Street for half a city block.

The Cloister - Glenwood Mission Inn, Riverside, California.

The Mission Wing and the Cloister Wing join near the leaded glass bay window.

suites of Authors Row, built of distinctive, reddish, hollow terra cotta blocks.

A small pedestrian bridge spans Sixth Street from the hotel to the Annex located across the street next to the underground guest parking facility. The Annex, now used for storage, was originally built as a dormitory for hotel employees who could walk to work across the bridge without going down to street level. Ceramic tiles inserted along the sides of the bridge depict Christopher Columbus, Queen Isabella, and various symbols of the New World.

Flying buttresses on Sixth and Orange streets are copied from the San Gabriel Mission. High above are the tower and dome patterned after the mission at Carmel.

24

A view of the massive Spanish and International Rotunda Wings on Sixth Street.

A decorative tile from the bridge over Sixth Street.

The bridge marks the end of the Spanish Wing and the beginning of the International Rotunda Wing, the last and most impressive of the additions to the Mission Inn. Designed by Riverside architect G. Stanley Wilson and named after the open cylindrical court which is 33 feet across and six stories high, construction began in 1929 and was completed in 1931. The Rotunda Wing starts with an arch-covered sidewalk along Sixth and Main streets. Rows of arched windows, round balconies, and a variety of tile and grille work adorn the upper levels. The majestic blue, gold, and white Amistad (Friendship) Dome crowns the corner of this section.

A variety of shops line the Main Street Mall, topped by office and professional suites with arched windows and

26

The majestic Amistad Dome crowns the corner of Sixth and Main streets.

wrought iron railings within the Rotunda Wing. The buttresses end where the Rotunda Wing gives way to the Mission Wing.

Mid-block, just beyond the end of the row of buttresses and marked by a small canopy, is a narrow corridor that leads from the city's Main Street Mall to the front entrance of the hotel. The first store on the corner of the corridor is occupied by the Inn-Credible Gift Corner, operated by the Friends of the Mission Inn. On the

Mission Inn shops line Riverside's Main Street Mall.

floors above the shops, more hotel rooms look out over the Mall, each with its distinctive doorway or decorative window. At the corner of the Mall and Mission Inn Avenue is the Mission Inn Foundation Museum, filled with many artifacts of an earlier Mission Inn.

Turning the corner from the Mission Inn Foundation Museum along Mission Inn Avenue, the sidewalk returns to the main entrance of the hotel.

COURT OF THE BIRDS

Pet macaws Napoleon and Joseph once greeted hotel guests near the entrance.

"It is a pity that the old padres never saw the advantage of founding a mission in Riverside. But since they did not, we will bring the most beautiful features of each of the missions right here."

— Frank Miller,
RIVERSIDE DAILY PRESS, 1909

The vine-covered *campanario*, a copy of the San Gabriel Mission belfry, towers high above the walkway leading from Mission Inn Avenue to the main entry doors of the hotel. Included in the 1902 Mission Wing project, it is one of the characteristic features typical of the early missions.

Frank Miller and guest admire the Nanking Bell.

Court of the Birds, Glenwood Mission Inn, Riverside, California.

The campanario marks the main entrance to the Mission Inn.

The Court of the Birds in the 1920s.

The beautiful tiled swimming pool, El Agua Azul, is located in the Court of the Birds.

When first constructed the *campanario* was attached to the original portion of the Glenwood known as the Old Adobe. A staircase built into the *campanario* led to a rooftop garden added to this building that had once served as the Miller family home.

In 1948 the Old Adobe was at last demolished and replaced with a large, heated swimming pool called El Agua Azul due to its blue-colored tiles. The refurbished pool and adjacent spa remain a popular area of the hotel.

Beyond the *campanario* lies the Court of the Birds, which resembles an old Spanish hacienda courtyard. This area is named for two Brazilian macaws owned by Isabella and Frank Miller. For many decades Joseph, with a coat of many colors, and Napoleon, with royal blue and gold feathers, perched daily beside the main entrance to the lobby. Although the birds neither talked nor flew after their wings were clipped, these colorful

greeters were favorites of many of the Inn's guests. Today images of Joseph and Napoleon are seen throughout the Mission Inn.

The U-shaped Mission Wing surrounds the Court of the Birds on three sides and is the oldest structure of the Mission Inn. Constructed in 1902, the four-story building was designed to resemble a California Mission. Over two hundred hotel rooms—no two alike—are reached by long corridors lined with oil paintings, antique furniture, and inset stained glass windows.

A row of rooms on the top floor opens onto a wide walkway that overlooks the Court of the Birds and downtown Riverside. On the ground floor are the Inn's public rooms which are filled with unusual art and artifacts from around the world.

A pergola of timbered cross beams and rafters supports a variety of flowering vines that provide shade to the walkways on three sides of the court-

A vine-covered pergola provides shade over the walkways.

The Mission Inn was designated a
National Historic Landmark in 1977.

yard. During the 1902 construction of the Mission Wing, the pergola was built of tree trunks and boughs. This arbor was subsequently replaced by a reinforced concrete replica which was itself replaced in 1985.

On the left side of the main entrance walk are two bronze Spanish cannons which had been part of the Philippine Exhibit at the 1915 San Francisco Panama Pacific International Exposition. The cannons, each weighing over a ton, arrived at the Mission Inn in December 1915. One is dated 1779 and the other 1814. At the close of the Exposition, Frank Miller purchased a large number of collectible objects including these cannons.

Two Spanish cannons stand near the walkway to the main entrance.

Today the Nanking Bell is housed in a protected portico.

The St. Francis Shrine is located along the walkway to the Main Street Mall.

Around the corner from the cannons sits the Nanking Bell. Now housed in a small free-standing portico, the bell came to Miller in 1914 as an addition to his collection of bells and crosses. This nineteenth-century cast bronze Chinese Temple Bell may have been the first Oriental art to make its way to the Inn in the aftermath of the Boxer Rebellion. Over one hundred years old, the bell's inscription dedicates it to the Temple of Heaven.

To the left of the hotel's main doors, the windows look into the hotel dining rooms, and the sidewalk leads past the pool to the shops on the Mall. A small memorial shrine to St. Francis is built into a triangular support column at the corner where the pergola continues around the inner court of the building.

Across the courtyard from the cannons stands a white gazebo, a recent addition to the Court of the Birds. The gazebo is situated between a bright blue fountain and a weathered rock waterfall. This lush, secluded setting is ideal for small gatherings and simple weddings.

Beyond the gazebo the waterfall cascades over rocks into a boulder-lined pool. Green sprouting bamboo, leafy shrubbery, and the soft sound of falling water envelope this sheltered spot. The tumbling water of the rock pool provides a backdrop for a stone statue of a regal woman and smaller sculptures half concealed in the swirling water. Partially hidden behind the fountain are several Spanish coats of arms and copies of pre-Aztec carved heads embedded in the brick wall.

The blue tile fountain in the Court of the Birds.

A decorative gazebo offers a secluded spot for small gatherings.

33

Upper: A small water-
fall cascades into a
boulder-lined pool.

Lower: The sculpture
of a regal woman
stands near the edge
of the pool.

The Court of the Birds was the site of an event of immense significance to Riverside's citrus heritage. On May 7, 1903, President Theodore Roosevelt visited the Mission Inn during his campaign for re-election. Before leaving Riverside the following morning to resume his tour, he participated in the ceremonial transplanting of a special tree in the courtyard of the Inn. The tree was one of two Brazilian navel orange trees that had been sent to Eliza and Luther Tibbets in 1873 from the Department of Agriculture in Washington, DC. These seedless orange trees became the parent rootstock for the

President Theodore Roosevelt transplanting one of the parent navel orange trees into the courtyard, May 8, 1903. Isabella and Frank Miller are to the right of the President.

navel orange industry. Cuttings from these two parent trees were grafted onto other citrus trees, establishing the basis of Riverside's horticultural economy.

The tree planted by President Roosevelt became such a tourist attraction that Frank Miller placed an iron fence around it for protection. Fruit from this tree was sent every year to the President until his death in 1919. The tree died shortly after and was replaced with one of its own descendants which still thrives in the Spanish Patio.

The other parent navel orange tree survives today in a small, triangular park at the corner of Magnolia and Arlington Avenues.

The carillon rises high above the main entrance to the Mission Inn.

GROUND FLOOR

"Entre, es su casa, amigo."

*"…the most unique hotel
in America.
It's a monastery,
a mission,
a fine hotel, a home,
a boarding house,
a museum, an art gallery
and an aviator's shrine."*

— Will Rogers, Humorist

*CALIFORNIA ALPS,
painted in 1874 by
California landscape
artist William Keith.*

The 94-foot-long lobby carpet features the 21 California Missions.

LOBBY

Outside the main entrance to the lobby is the Mission Inn escutcheon with the figures of St. Francis of Assisi and Father Junipero Serra. A California Indian, along with bells and crosses, represents the missions. Beneath the figures is the inscription, *"Entre, es su casa, amigo,"* the traditional welcome to homes in Spain and Mexico.

Inside the lobby is an impressive expanse of dark beam ceilings, tall stucco wall arches, and massive wooden pillars lining the long corridor. While some alterations have been made to the lobby to meet the changing needs of the times, most of the original Mission style design elements remain.

High on the wall, just past the reception desk, hangs the magnificent painting *California Alps* by noted Scottish-American artist William Keith. One of the Inn's most valuable possessions, this impressive six-by-eight-foot oil on canvas was painted in 1874. Considered Keith's first grand epic painting, *California Alps* is a harmonious combination of several scenes blended together to form a portrait of the natural beauty of California's Sierra Nevada range.

The background of the painting shows jagged peaks rising above snow fields and glaciers. Below is weathered granite with canyons and crevices worn into the resisting stone. Two waterfalls cascade down canyon walls into a tumbling river. The vegetation is correct in color and detail and typical of the canyon flanks. In the foreground, in

contrast to the epic scale of the scenery, are figures of California Indians, going about their daily chores. Keith toured the Sierra Nevadas with the noted naturalist, John Muir, sketching with such careful attention to detail that Muir later called this painting "the bible of the Sierras."

Today the lobby furnishings are a blend of antiques and Oriental pieces.

Below the Keith painting is the smaller oil *Arch Beach* dated 1918 and signed by William Wendt, a noted artist of the California Impressionist School. Wendt earned a national reputation for his dreamy landscapes of the canyons and shoreline near his Laguna Beach home on the coast of Orange County, California.

The lobby stretches toward Orange Street for half a city block with conversational areas scat-

Upper: The Centennial piano was manufactured in 1875 by the Steinway Company of New York; Middle right: Actor and pianist Dudley Moore plays the Steinway Centennial on a visit to the Mission Inn.

President Taft's oversized chair is a favorite tourist attraction.

tered around the fireplace and throughout the long corridor. A 94-foot carpet, featuring the likeness and name of each of the 21 California Missions arranged by founding dates, provides an intriguing path through the lobby.

Originally furnished with simple, uncluttered furnishings in keeping with the Mission theme, the lobby has undergone many transformations. Today handsome antique and Oriental pieces blend with more contemporary accessories; Victorian elegance harmonizes with vividly patterned Oriental area carpets and throw rugs.

A most unusual grand piano rests in a place of honor. When repairs were made to the piano in 1986, a serial number etched into the sounding board revealed that it was manufactured in 1875 by the Steinway Company of New York in honor of the United States Centennial in 1876. After 1876 Steinway lost track of the piano. How and when it arrived at the Mission Inn is a mystery.

In 1909 at Frank Miller's direction, an oversized chair was built by Inn carpenters for President William Howard

The elegant lobby is filled with artifacts, statues and art.

Taft in anticipation of a grand banquet in his honor. Carved into the wide wooden crossbar above the back of the padded seat are the words "President Taft's Chair" and the date "October 12, 1909." Even though the President weighed 335 pounds, the chair was so generous in size that during the banquet Taft is rumored to have asked, "Did you have to make the chair so large?" The famous wooden Taft chair is a favorite attraction where visitors often stop and have their pictures taken.

The entrance to the Presidential Lounge is through decorative grille gates from the lobby.

PRESIDENTIAL LOUNGE

ronze gates frame the entrance into the interior of the Presidential Lounge. A heavy beam ceiling and dark paneled walls are brightened by an unusual skylight dome of blue and gold stained glass. To commemorate President Roosevelt's May 7, 1903 visit, the stained glass window facing the Court of the Birds displays the Presidential flag and date.

The Presidential Lounge was originally built in 1902 as a luxurious four-room apartment. President Theodore Roosevelt stayed in the apartment during his overnight visit in 1903, and

A stained glass replica of the Presidential flag commemorates President Theodore Roosevelt's 1903 visit.

President William Howard Taft enjoyed the seclusion of the Suite in 1909 before attending the grand banquet. In 1926 Crown Prince Gustavus and Princess Louise of Sweden occupied the suite briefly before being escorted to a festive dinner party in the outdoor Spanish Patio.

By 1939 the apartment had been converted into a large room suitable for meetings or other functions. In 1940 Richard Nixon and Patricia Ryan were married in a simple Quaker ceremony on June 21. The space was remodeled in 1957 into a cocktail lounge and completely renovated again during the 1985 restoration.

42

The Presidential Lounge was originally a large four-room apartment built as part of the Mission Wing in 1902.

In the lobby adjacent to the Presidential Lounge are portraits of Presidents who have visited the Inn during their lifetime. These were copied by artist Bonnie Brown from the official White House portraits.

Today drinks are also served in a lobby area adjacent to the cocktail lounge. On the wall are portraits of Presidents of the United States who have visited the Mission Inn during their lifetimes. Only three, Benjamin Harrison, Theodore Roosevelt, and William Howard Taft, stopped at the Inn while in office.

One of two small stained glass windows in the Presidential Lounge.

CLOISTER MUSIC ROOM

cross the lobby from the Presidential Lounge and behind double doors are steps leading down to the Cloister Music Room, the largest public room in the Mission Inn. The Music Room played an important role in the story of the Mission Inn as the scene of daily music recitals and sing-a-longs until the late 1940s. It also hosted—and continues to host—a variety of public functions: operas, concerts, seminars, and other large gatherings.

Built in 1910 as part of architect Arthur B. Benton's design for the Cloister Wing, the floor of the room is a half-story below ground level. The rough hewn beams and the balcony were copied from California's Mission San Miguel. Originally the architecture was augmented with Spanish

The Music Room is often used for wedding receptions, business dinners or other large gatherings.

The imposing Music Room is the largest public room in the Mission Inn.

paintings, tapestries, arms, armor, and flags decorating the walls and hanging from the balcony. Pew benches, some of which remain at the rear of the room, were copied from those in Westminster Abbey and installed along the east and south walls.

During the planning phase of the Cloister Wing, Miller's wife Isabella died after a long illness. In her honor, Miller commissioned artisan Harry Eldridge Goodhue to memorialize her in stained glass. The three-panel window brings light to the Music Room stage at the north end of the room. Isabella Miller is depicted as St. Cecilia, the patroness saint of music, seated at an organ in the window's center panel. Joseph, Mrs. Miller's favorite of the hotel's macaws, appears with her.

The 1910 Cloister Music Room was built as an entertainment center for hotel guests.

The hotel's *campanario* provides a background.

The right panel pictures three Franciscan nuns in front of the Old Adobe, the Miller family's

45

original dwelling. The panel on the left side shows three Franciscan friars under a pergola much like the Inn's original vine-covered arbor. Other stained glass pieces are installed in the windows facing Orange Street.

To the right of the Music Room stage is a Kilgen pipe organ. Originally installed when the Cloister Wing was built, the organ was electrified and refurbished in 1930.

The Music Room was also Frank Miller's first venture into gallery space specifically designed to exhibit his art collection. Some of the closed arches on the east side of the room originally opened into the Cloister Walk, more popularly known as the Catacombs. Miller filled the walls with paintings, some of which he purchased for the general area and others that he commissioned with a specific location in mind.

The Catacombs also included niches built into the poured concrete to hold statues of Catholic saints. The gallery space in the Catacombs was later enlarged to accommodate the Miller family's ever-increasing collection of American, European, and Asian paintings and sculpture. In addition large areas were devoted to Native American Indian basketry and textiles. Of special interest was a small room housing the Papal Court lifelike wax figures of Pope Pius X and his 13 attendants.

The Catacombs are no longer used for display and are currently closed to the public for safety reasons.

The center stained glass window at the back of the stage depicts Isabella Miller as St. Cecilia, the patroness saint of music.

Actress Ginger Rogers and other dignitaries served on the National Advisory Commission of the Mission Inn.

The Cloister Walk, popularly known as the Catacombs, was built to display the Miller collection of artifacts.

For many years a Papal Court of 14 lifelike wax figures was housed in the Catacombs.

The St. Francis doors, crafted of bronze and iron, open into the California Lounge.

CALIFORNIA LOUNGE AND DINING ROOMS

Beyond the *California Alps* and *Arch Beach* paintings and the elevator doors edged in bright tiles, the lobby becomes the spacious California Lounge. This room can be closed off from the lobby by two intricately crafted, bronze and iron doors depicting episodes from the life of St. Francis. The central parts of the St. Francis doors are open-work screens of wrought iron, with birds perched in twining tendrils of foliage.

Past the St. Francis doors and down two steps into the California Lounge, a round, ornamental floor mosaic features the Millers' two pet macaws, Napoleon and Joseph.

The lounge area, part of the oldest section of the hotel, has many features that reflect the early

A mosaic floor medallion features the Mission Inn macaws, Napoleon and Joseph.

Mission style of the building. High arched windows, dark beam ceilings, brick-faced walls, and antique-appearing wall sconces carry out the theme.

At the far end of the California Lounge is the Inn's most exclusive dining area, Duane's Prime Steaks, named for Duane Roberts, owner of the Mission Inn. The elegant atmosphere of Duane's is enhanced by a dramatic painting prominently displayed on the center panel of the brick wall.

The massive painting, dated 1900, features one of the Inn's most famous guests, President Theodore Roosevelt. Painted by Russian artist Vasilli V. Vereschagin, the oil on canvas measures 95 inches by 68 inches with a 12-inch gilt wood frame.

A replica of the famous sculpture The Thorn Puller is prominently displayed in the California Lounge.

Vereshchagin was best known for his epic war scenes of Europe's famous battles. In 1899 the artist visited America and met Theodore Roosevelt, recently returned from the Spanish American War. Roosevelt related the incidents of San Juan Hill which Vereschagin then painted.

Roosevelt, who had been lauded in the American newspapers for his daring under fire, must have appreciated

The elaborate Sunday brunch is an enjoyable feature of the Mission Inn Dining Room.

The Mission Inn's talented chefs present a sumptuous cuisine.

Vereshchagin's painting because he used a copy to illustrate his book *The Rough Riders* published in 1900. That same year the painting was exhibited at the Chicago Institute of Art where it was purchased for $1800 by a Northern California art collector. In 1917 Frank Miller attended an auction in San Francisco and returned to Riverside with this and several other paintings to add to his growing collection at the Mission Inn.

Within Duane's Prime Steaks, is the separate Frank Miller Executive Dining Room. Furnished with prized antiques and fine paintings, the Frank Miller Room is the site of corporate dinners and gatherings when privacy in elegant surroundings is desired.

Hovsep Pushman's 1918 portrait, *Frank A. Miller, Master of the Mission Inn,* looks gravely over the room. On the wall across from Miller is the lovely portrait *Allis Miller, Daughter of the Inn*. In 1909 Miller commissioned noted mid-west artist

One of the Inn's exclusive dining areas is Duane's Prime Steaks.

Named for Duane Roberts, the owner of the hotel, Duane's provides elegant dining surrounded by art.

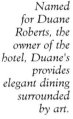

SAN JUAN HILL painted in 1900 by Russian artist Vasilli Vereshchagin features Theodore Roosevelt and his Rough Riders in the most famous battle of the Spanish American War

The Frank Miller Executive Dining Room is furnished with antique furniture and fine paintings.

OUR LADY OF THE
ANGELS BLESSING
THE CITY OF
LOS ANGELES.
*A painting by George
Melville Stone.*

ST. BARBARA ON
THE HILL ABOVE
THE MISSION AT
SANTA BARBARA.
*A painting by George
Melville Stone.*

The Mission Inn Restaurant was formerly known as the Spanish Dining Room.

George Melville Stone to paint Allis at the Mission Inn. Mr. Stone and his wife spent a month in a suite of rooms in the hotel, one of which was used as his studio.

Pleased with the painting of his daughter, Miller engaged Stone to paint a series of California Mission paintings for the Mission Inn. Stone eventually produced more than 20 paintings, several of which now hang in the Frank Miller Room.

Actress Judy Garland and husband David Rose dine in the Spanish Patio in 1941.

Another dining room adjacent to the lounge area is the Mission Inn Restaurant, originally called the Spanish Dining Room. Constructed in 1915 as a part of the Spanish Wing, architect Myron Hunt designed the room to resemble a banquet hall in a Spanish castle. Distinctive features of this room are the walls and support pillars of imported ceramic tiles that incorporate a variety of textures and colors. Painted crescent-shaped lunettes are set into the broad arches above the doors that lead to the Spanish Patio.

THE SPANISH PATIO

The Anton Clock tower contains five rotating figures symbolic of California's history and the Mission Inn.

The Spanish Patio, designed to represent a castle's inner court, became an open-air dining room upon completion of the Spanish Wing. The Patio is equipped for year-round dining comfort and offers *al fresco* meals in one of the most delightful areas of the Inn.

Frank Miller's plans for the Spanish Patio originated from his 1911 visit to Spain. Terra cotta tiles cover the floor, and the entire west wall was inspired by a visit to Seville. The central water fountain that features four grinning gargoyles was originally the crown of a municipal fountain at Cordova, while some of the tile came from Triana, the tile works in Seville. The gargoyles were made at the Inn, copied from a water spout brought by the Millers to the Inn from the battlement of a castle near Barcelona. Tiers of balconies with wrought iron railings overlook the enclosed patio.

In the northwest corner of the patio, the Anton Clock tower, two-stories high, presents five rotating figures symbolic of California's history. Father Serra, Juan Bautista de Anza, St. Francis, the California grizzly bear, and a California Indian were designed to revolve on the quarter hour, but often turn at will. The clock face is a replica of the 1709 wooden original from Nuremburg, Germany, which is on permanent display in the Mission Inn

An early view of the landscaped Spanish Patio.

Museum. Painted on the wall beneath the clock is a favorite saying of Frank Miller's from Proverbs (29:18): "Where there is no vision, the people perish."

Below the Anton Clock, a navel orange tree, grafted from the Inn's transplanted parent tree, spreads its branches over the northwest corner of the patio.

Rising high above the south wall is the carillon where favorite traditional melodies are frequently played, and the melodic chimes ring out over the busy hotel and city streets. For many years a song by Carrie Jacobs Bond—*A Perfect Day*—was played every evening about sunset. Mrs. Bond was a frequent guest at the Inn and wrote the song here after touring the area with friends. She is also known for composing the wedding favorite, *I Love You Truly.*

Weathered tiles cover the floor and surround a large central water fountain featuring four grinning gargoyles.

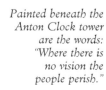

Random tiles are installed along a wall of the Spanish Patio.

In 1926, Prince Gustavus and Princess Louise of Sweden attended an elegant banquet in their honor in the Spanish Patio.

56

Painted beneath the Anton Clock tower are the words: "Where there is no vision the people perish."

Evening dining in the Spanish Patio is an experience long remembered.

Diners are entertained in the Spanish Patio.

Walls surrounding the Spanish Patio hold a variety of flags, plaques and images.

Spanish Patio, Glenwood Mission Inn, Riverside, California.

Dining al fresco in the early days.

THE SPANISH ART GALLERY

At the north end of the Spanish Patio, broad marble steps lead to an old Spanish door that opens into the Spanish Art Gallery. The centuries-old door features a carved pomegranate, the emblem of Granada.

The Spanish Art Gallery in the Spanish Wing opened on New Year's Eve, 1914, with a formal gala attended by hundreds of guests. Construction on the two-story art gallery, the focal point in the new wing, had begun in the spring of 1912. Designed by

The Spanish Art Gallery was designed to display the Miller family's growing collection of European art.

Glenwood Mission Inn, Riverside, California.

A 1917 postcard looking toward the west end of the Spanish Art Gallery.

Pasadena architect Myron Hunt to house the vast accumulation of paintings and artifacts collected by the Miller family, the gallery was reminiscent of the salons of seventeenth-century Europe. The room's great height and proportions were enhanced by the draped canopied ceiling, wrought iron railings, and oversized windows.

For many years the Spanish Art Gallery was home to a large collection of old and valued paintings. The Mission Inn art collection featured some originals and copies of famous old masters such as Raphael, Rubens, and Botticelli. Many of the paintings that found a permanent home at the Mission Inn were

THE LOST CHORD, a study in brown by
the German artist Gabriel Schachinger.

THE LOST CHORD, a study in brown by
the German artist Gabriel Schachinger.

This early eighteenth century Italian painting,
THE BEGGAR, is attributed to artist
Antonio Amorosi.

FLIGHT INTO EGYPT
by Gaspar de Craeyer.

first introduced in exhibits in the Spanish Art Gallery.

As his interest in art expanded, Frank Miller found ways to increase his collection. He added more Spanish art and, in 1917, a collection of Russian paintings. Traditional religious art and images, early California mission paintings, scenes of California Indian life, and more modern paintings followed. In 1920 the massive proportions of the Spanish Art Gallery allowed the Rayas Altar from Mexico to be housed here before it was moved to the St. Francis Chapel.

During construction of the International Rotunda Wing in 1931, Riverside architect G. Stanley Wilson was presented with the problem of connecting the new addition to the Spanish Art Gallery. His solution was to have his associate, Albert Haight, design the handsome marble stairway leading to a small room called the Signature Room, which exits into the St. Francis Atrio in the Rotunda Wing. After a wedding ceremony in the St. Francis Chapel, bridal couples may cross the Atrio, pause in the Signature Room to sign their names, then step through the doorway for

Spanish Altar, Glenwood Mission Inn, Riverside, California.

A view toward the east end of the gallery where the gold altar was first displayed.

MISSION INN, RIVERSIDE, CALIFORNIA—4

Installed in 1931, a marble staircase connects the Spanish Art Gallery to the Signature Room and the St. Francis Atrio.

Following tradition, a bridal couple makes their grand entrance, then descends the marble staircase after their wedding in the St. Francis Chapel.

a graceful descent down the double stairway to their wedding reception in the Gallery.

Another feature of the Spanish Art Gallery is the stained glass art windows, designed by Jessie Van Brunt to honor the Miller family. Of special interest is the one in memory of Frank Miller's sister, Alice Richardson, depicting St. Martha, patroness saint of hospitality.

While the Spanish Art Gallery has undergone some changes, it remains basically as it was originally conceived: a long, high-walled room intended for exhibiting paintings and other art. Owner Duane Roberts and the Friends of the Mission Inn have restored much of the fine old art that remains in the Inn's collection. At present almost 100 paintings and art works adorn the gallery walls.

The bulk of the California mission paintings

The Spanish Art Gallery decorated for a wedding reception.

The memorial window of St. Martha, patroness saint of hospitality, honors Alice Miller Richardson, Manager of the Inn for over fifty years.

by Henry Chapman Ford—36 small oils on canvas—are found in this room. After settling in Santa Barbara around 1870, Ford became fascinated by the California missions and painted them before any restoration work occurred. Ford's career is almost exclusively defined by his studies of these early missions; his work is a reliable historical record of the condition of the missions in the late 1800s. After Ford's death in 1894, Frank Miller purchased 38

This window of St. Cecilia, the patroness saint of music, was originally a feature of the Saint Cecilia Oratory, the first "wedding" chapel in the Mission Inn.

paintings for the Mission Inn. Of this series, two were lost to decay or damage from flooding, and the remaining canvases comprise a historic collection of mission paintings.

At present the Spanish Art Gallery can be reserved for wedding receptions and other large gatherings.

The Spanish Art Gallery is an impressive room, often used for large meetings or gatherings.

Carmel Mission; SAN CARLOS BORROMEO De CARMELO

CALIFORNIA MISSION PAINTINGS *by Henry Chapman Ford. Henry Chapman Ford began painting the California Missions in 1870. His studies included water color sketches, oils, and etchings of the rapidly decaying missions.*

San Gabriel Mission; SAN GABRIEL ARCANGEL

FIRST FLOOR

*"It is unbelievable,
it is the
spirit of California,
imprisoned."*

— *Actress Lillian Russell*

*FRAY JUNIPERO SERRA AND
DON GASPAR De PORTOLA AT
MONTEREY BAY, JUNE 3, 1770,
one of three story oils painted by
James E. McBurney for the Mission Inn.*

Artist James E. McBurney told the story of the founding of the
California missions on three large canvases for the Mission
Inn. Designed to fit into the large arched niches of the arcade
leading to the Spanish Art Gallery, the canvases were stretched
over wood supports to be hung without frames.

Sold at the 1957 auction of Mission Inn art and antiques, two
of the paintings were purchased and returned for display at the
hotel by the Friends of the Mission Inn in 1985. Both canvases
were severely damaged and required restoration and repair,
which was funded by the Friends in 1994.

GOING UP...

The floors of the Mission Inn are designated in European fashion with the street level lobby considered the ground floor, and the first level up, the first floor.

The first floor of the hotel is reached by elevator or by walking up the main staircase that begins near the reception desk. From the balcony of the first landing, visitors are rewarded with a different view of the William Keith painting of the *California Alps* in the lobby. Since the painting is so large, much of the imagery is lost in the view from the ground floor. From the balcony the mountains and waterfalls are even more glorious, and the fine details of the Indian village scene can be fully appreciated.

At the top of the stairs is a large unframed oil painting with a curved top. This was one of the three paintings by James E. McBurney commissioned by Frank Miller for the Mission Inn. Painted in 1912 and 1913, the unframed oils were specifically designed to fit the arched niches of the Spanish Art Gallery's sheltered arcade.

The McBurney paintings tell the story of the founding of the California Missions, a history lesson in oils. All three of the McBurney paintings were sold at the 1957 Ben Swig auction of

Spacious guest rooms, furnished with elegance and comfort contrast with the original Arts and Crafts style furnishings of the earlier Mission Inn hotel rooms.

GLENWOOD MISSION INN RIVERSIDE, CALIFORNIA.

C-109

THE GOOD SAMARITAN, painted in 1904 by Russian artist Professor N. A. Kosscheloff.

Mission Inn art and artifacts and considered lost to the hotel collection. In 1985 a Riverside antique dealer notified the Friends of the Mission Inn that two of the McBurney paintings had been located and were for sale. *Fray Junipero Serra Praying for the Return of the Relief Ship to San Diego* and *Fray Junipero Serra and Don Gaspar de Portola at Monterey Bay* were purchased by the Friends. The third painting, *Fray Junipero Serra Meeting With the California Indians* is still missing.

At the west end of the first floor corridor, a colorful stained glass window richly decorated with jewels fused to glass, honors St. Chad, the Bishop of Lichfield. This seventh century English missionary traveled on foot throughout the countryside preaching the gospel and is credited with converting the Anglo Saxons from paganism to Christianity.

A narrow hallway to the right of the elevator leads to an outside exit and a balcony overlooking the Spanish Patio. All four wings of the Mission Inn are visible from here.

ST. CHAD
Gleaming with jewel-like colors, a handsome stained glass window pays tribute to the seventh century English missionary St. Chad, the Bishop of Lichfield.

The Spanish
Patio wa.
inspired by
the Millers
trip to
Spain

OVERLOOK

Along the eastern side of the Spanish Patio, above the first floor, is an open rooftop section known as the Garden of the Bells. A row of arches, anchored on the left by a mission bell tower, holds a variety of historic bells. Members of the Miller family accumulated over 800 bells from all over the world, some of great historic value and others of religious significance.

The southernmost arch houses the oldest dated bell in Christendom. Its inscription reads, "James, Jesus Christ, Mary: Quintana and Salvador made me in the year of our Lord 1247." Frank Miller discovered this bell when he visited the foundry that produced the original chimes for Big Ben in London. Miller wandered into a room containing a large jumble of bells. Two of them caught his eye; he paid the $25 asking price and requested the foundry hold his purchases until he was ready to go home.

When Frank Miller returned for his bells, he was informed that the inscribed bell had been promised to the British Museum. With his bill of sale in hand, Miller complained to the head of the British Museum, who finally agreed that, since the bell was Spanish and not English in the first place, it belonged to Miller and thus to the Mission Inn.

The Ramona Dome, a small replica of the dome at Mission San Juan Capistrano presided over by a marble statue of St. Francis of Assisi.

The Anton Clock tower, as it appeared in 1943 with statues in the tall arched openings. The moving figures seen today were added a decade later.

The delicate blue and white della Robbia is a reproduction of a famous original found in Florence, Italy.

A wreath of oak leaves, and stag's head with antlers symbolize the conversion of St. Hubert, the patron saint of hunters.

The Spanish explorer Juan Bautista de Anza, one of five historic figures that turn with the clock's movement.

On the walls surrounding the Spanish Patio, randomly placed tiles feature coats of arms. Intermingled with the tiles are blue and white della Robbias and, in a far corner, a wreath circling a stag's head commemorates St. Hubert's conversion to Christianity. An unfinished fresco by Italian artist A. G. Disi, a graduate of the Art Academy of Rome, depicts Mission Inn symbols on the wall near the Anton Clock.

A rich panorama of balconies, arches, shadowed doorways, domes, red roof tiles, iron railings, open corridors, and covered walkways stretch off in all directions, blending the inspirational and international design elements of this fascinating hotel.

The original carved wood face of the Anton Clock is on display in the Mission Inn Museum.

Upper and lower Oriental Court as it was originally designed.

COURT OF THE ORIENT

In the 1920s and 1930s Frank Miller amassed a collection of Oriental art. Miller traveled extensively and purchased art wherever he went, including the Orient, Los Angeles, and San Francisco. As his interest in the Far East grew, the collection filled several rooms on the first floor of the Mission Inn and was eventually moved to the Court of the Orient.

After Miller's death in 1935 and during the years of the Second World War, Allis Miller Hutchings and her husband DeWitt converted the lower level of the Court of the Orient to the Lea Lea Room, a Polynesian nightclub. The bulk of the Oriental collection was housed here and in the adjacent Ho-O-Kan room. The 1985 restoration returned the Court of the Orient to its original proportions. Much of the collection is now distributed throughout the Inn and the Mission Inn Museum, with the remainder in storage.

The present day Court of the Orient is entered through what was formerly called the Hall of the Gods. Some of the changes that have occurred in this portion of the Mission Inn are illustrated in photographs on the wall.

Outside the Hall is the Court

Gilt and red lacquer demonic statue made between the late eighteenth and early nineteenth centuries.

The Lea Lea Room—Hawaiian for 'Room of Laughter'—was in existence from 1939 until 1985.

of the Orient, with Oriental lanterns and marble steps that lead to the upper level. Today this area is used for dinners, small weddings, and other gatherings. Double doors open into the Ho-O-Kan room, originally designed as a shrine to house the *Amitabha* Buddha. Over the Ho-O-Kan doors reigns the *Mandarin's Journey,* a carving made from a single piece of wood depicting a mandarin and his entourage on a trek up the mountain to seek spiritual solace from a hermit.

Stepping through the Ho-O-Kan doors, visitors are greeted by an eight and one-half foot *Amitabha* Buddha. This serene figure was made in Japan during the Tokugawa period (1615-1868) of wood, gilt, and lacquer. The figure sits on an eight-sided lotus blossom, symbolizing the lotus rising from a murky pond in its pristine whiteness, just as the Buddha rises out of the murky world in all his purity.

The elongated ears show that the actual Buddha was born a prince who gave up his regal trimmings to search for enlightenment. Other symbols include the *urna,* a white curl between his eyes facing the right, from which emanates the light illuminating the universe. In his head is the *ushnisha* or crystal ball symbolizing wisdom and enlightenment. Hand gestures are known as *mudras,* and this one is the *mudra* of meditation.

Also in the Ho-O-Kan Room is *Riui,* an eight-foot bronze dragon. He holds a bowl which may have contained water or a precious stone originally, and his tail curls around to serve as the base on which he stands. Dragons in the Orient are benign creatures, and when they have five claws, they are reserved for the emperor. This dragon has but four.

Many items from the Oriental Collection are now found in the Mission Inn Museum.

Upper and lower Oriental Court as it appears today.

74

In the Ho-O-Kan Room, the eight-and-a-half-foot Amitabha Buddha sits serenely on an eight-sided lotus blossom.

St. Francis Atrio

A step around the corner into the St. Francis Atrio is a step back into Spanish Colonial Mexico. Across the travertine flagstones, the huge portal entrance to the St. Francis Chapel seems to dominate until the myriad details of balconies, steps, wrought iron, glazed tile, and the carved facades of this romantic space come into focus. In the center of the Atrio, spewing water, sits a bronze statue of the Greek god Bacchus, a copy of the Bacchus fountain in Prato, Italy.

The travertine tiled courtyard called the Atrio is one of the most majestic areas of the Mission Inn.

Above the large wooden doors of the chapel, Our Lady of Guadalupe stands in bas-relief flanked by two round emblems. On her right is the coat of arms of the Franciscan order, and on her left, that of the College of San Fernando, the Franciscan monastery in Mexico City where Fray Junipero Serra lived and worked before his long journey to California. Higher is a large, round Tiffany window, and still higher, almost at the top of the building, a small white statue of St. Francis stands under a circle of birds, representing the gentle saint preaching to the birds.

To the left of the portal, behind a wrought-iron gate, are the copper wings of the Famous Fliers' Wall, each honoring a noted flier who visited the Inn. This

One of the original drawings by the talented artist William A. Sharp, an associate of architect Arthur B. Benton.

78

Made of copper, the wings measure about 10 inches across.

tradition originated with Frank Miller's daughter Allis and son-in-law DeWitt Hutchings in 1934. Famous fliers who came by invitation or just happened to be at the Inn were honored at a special, sometimes elaborate, ceremony at the

From left: Movie stars Charles Drake, Robert Cummings and Don DeFore pose with Isabella Hutchings, DeWitt Hutchings and Allis Miller Hutchings.

Fliers' Wall. After appropriate speeches and introductions, usually orchestrated by consummate master of ceremonies DeWitt Hutchings, the honoree tacked to the Wall a pair of copper wings with his or her autograph etched into the left wing and the date of the ceremony on the right. Etched between the wings is a symbol, date, or phrase apropos of the flier.

World War II Air Corps Chief of Staff, Hap Arnold, was an old friend of DeWitt Hutchings. Arnold had the Army shield worked into the center of his wings, as did several other early Army fliers, including Jimmy Doolittle. World War

I ace, Eddie Rickenbacker, chose "Eastern Airlines," as he was president of the company at the time of his ceremony in 1942. Amelia Earhart simply put "A. E." The tradition continues today long after the deaths of Allis and DeWitt Hutchings in the early fifties. One hundred forty-five wings cover the Wall, the last placed in 1997 by Guadalcanal hero and later Governor of South Dakota, Joe Foss, who participated in a dual ceremony with Vietnam ace and San Diego Congressman, Randy "Duke" Cunningham.

In front of the Fliers' Wall stands another statue of St. Francis with a deer and wolf—mortal enemies coexisting at the saint's knee. At the opening of the Atrio is a nativity scene in della Robbia style blue and yellow ceramic.

To the right of the portal is the door to the Galeria, traditionally an art gallery, now housing an assortment of statuary gathered from forgotten corners and niches throughout the Inn. Past the Galeria door at the corner, begins the St. Joseph Arcade which extends the

General Henry "Hap" Arnold, later Commander-in-Chief of the Air Force in World War II, in front of the Fliers' Wall in 1936.

length of the outside wall to the door of the tiny St. Cecilia Wedding Chapel. Under the Arcade

Plaque dedicating the chapel to
St. Francis.

Senator John Glenn of Ohio, the first American to orbit the earth, added his wings to the
Fliers' Wall in 1982.

A view of the St. Francis Chapel and Atrio in 1931 before the Fliers' Wall was established.

This cerami
della Robbi
style ba
relief of th
nativity scen
flanked b
St. Catherin
and St
Barbar
(holding he
tower) is date
1522, but i
likely a lat
nineteenth o
early twentiet
century cop

SANCTA
BARBERA

SALVEVIRGOP ARENSTERRARVMCV NIAREGENTIS
SALVESPESHO MINVMGRATIAV ITASALVS
QVESTODEVOTO TABERNACHOLOAN O FATTOFAREGIVOMI
DELREAMEDIBEL TEME POST O INV IASANCTACHATERINA
MDXXII

SANCTA
CHATERIA

A small statue of St. Francis surveys the Atrio from the niche near the top of the chapel facade.

are panels of stained glass showing three scenes of Christ in the temple and to the left, the Frank Miller Memorial Window. Installed after his death in 1935, this window features Miller in Franciscan robes with outstretched arms surrounded by the symbols of the great religions of the world. Frank Miller welcomed all to his hotel and to his chapel.

The emphasis on St. Francis at the Inn came about after the Millers traveled to Italy in 1906, where they visited Assisi and heard the stories of the founder of the Franciscan Order. After returning home, Miller designated the famous saint as the patron saint of the Mission Inn. Years later in 1931, when Miller completed his last building project, the International Rotunda Wing which includes the Atrio, he named this space after St. Francis. *Atrio* is a Spanish word that refers to an enclosed open-air area in front of a church. Miller used the word appropriately because behind the great wooden portal doors is the chapel, also named after and dedicated to St. Francis.

The center panel
of the three Gothic
windows of
CHRIST IN
THE TEMPLE
made by Gorham
Studios.

This bronze statue
of St. Francis by
Ruth Sherwood
stands in a
special shrine
in the Atrio.

A memorial art
glass window
honors Frank
Miller's tolerance
for people of all
races and
religions.

The gold of the reredos and the jewel-toned Tiffany windows create a rich palette of colors in the softly lit chapel.

ST. FRANCIS CHAPEL

J n an elaborate ceremony in 1931, the chapel was formally dedicated to St. Francis of Assisi and identified as an International Shrine to Aviators. The latter designation reflected the Miller family's interest in aviation, particularly that of Miller's daughter Allis and her husband DeWitt Hutchings.

A Catholic Monsignor from Los Angeles presided over the

The pews are decorated with carved images of saints.

dedication ceremony although the chapel is non-denominational. Frank Miller was, in fact, a Congregationalist who welcomed guests of all religions to his chapel.

The great gold Rayas Altar screen dominates the usually dimly-lit interior. This eighteenth century treasure was created over 200 years ago for the private chapel in the home of the wealthy Rayas family in

Made in the 1700s of carved Mexican cedar, and covered by several thicknesses of gold leaf, the reredos was constructed in sections and fastened together with wooden pegs.

St. Joseph, patron saint of brides, stands above the cross in the glass case of the reredos.

Guanajuato, Mexico. In the early twentieth century, the Rayas family fortune was depleted and the home sold. Upon the recommendation of a friend, Frank Miller bought the reredos, as such an altar screen is called, sight unseen in 1920. For ten years the screen resided in the Spanish Art Gallery until Miller's talented workmen installed it in the Chapel's custom-designed alcove in 1931.

The elaborately carved details of the gold leaf covered surfaces and the numerous saints reflect the Mexican Baroque style of decorative art popular in Mexico during the eighteenth and nineteenth centuries. St. Joseph stands above the cross in the glass

Entitled ST. FRANCIS AND THE FLYING CROSS, this 18th century Mexican painting by an unknown artist depicts St. Francis receiving the stigmata, the wounds of Christ, after seeing a vision of the crucified Christ flying through the sky.

Setting an appropriate theme for weddings, THE MARRIAGE OF MARY AND JOSEPH is often referred to as "The Espousal of the Virgin." Painted on wood, it is attributed to Spanish artist Baltazar de Echave.

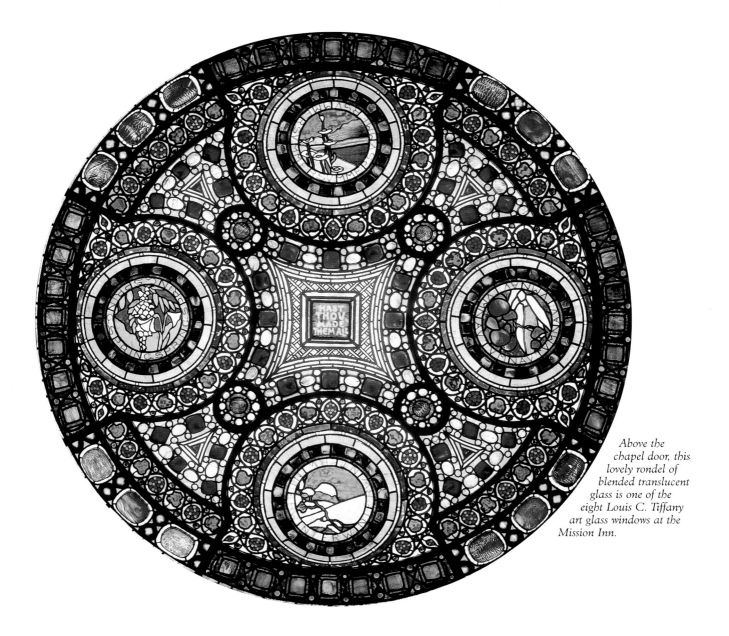

Above the chapel door, this lovely rondel of blended translucent glass is one of the eight Louis C. Tiffany art glass windows at the Mission Inn.

case. He is the patron saint of brides, which is appropriate, for this is a wedding chapel. No regular religious services are conducted here, but thousands of brides have walked down the aisle to stand at the base of the reredos and take their vows under the benevolent and protective gaze of St. Joseph.

Frank Miller obtained the chapel's stained glass windows about the same time as the Rayas Altar. America's greatest glass

Tiffany rondel undergoing restoration.

maker, Louis Comfort Tiffany, designed and made the windows in 1906 for architect Stanford White's masterpiece, the Madison Square Presbyterian Church in New York City. New owners tore down the church just 13 years later, and the windows were returned to Tiffany. A former visitor to the Inn, Tiffany contacted Miller who purchased them and placed them in storage for over ten years. In 1931 Miller installed seven of the Tiffany windows in

A view of the Atrio as seen through the high arched doorway of the St. Francis Chapel.

Bette Davis and William Grant Sherry were married in the St. Francis Chapel on November 29, 1945.

his new chapel and one on the western wall of the Galeria next door.

The large, round window, or "rondel," over the door is transparent as are the three tall, vertical panels seen on the left when entering the chapel. For the three panels on the right, Tiffany used special opaque glass designed to reflect light. As the eyes adjust to the dim light, parts of these panels begin to glow. For both sets of panels, the large circles down the center feature scenes from the Bible, while the smaller circles on the outside edges represent various months of the year with snow scenes, harvest scenes, flowers, and fruit.

*The same view of the Galeria,
separated by decades.*

GALERIA

The Galeria, a long, narrow room with a 30-foot ceiling, shares a common wall with the St. Francis Chapel. Completed in 1931, this room originally was used as an art gallery for the Millers' expanding art collection. Two of the important pieces displayed here were *San Juan Hill*, the massive painting that shows the charge up San Juan Hill, now in Duane's Prime Steaks, and William Keith's *California Alps*, now in the main lobby.

Now the Galeria is often the locale of wedding receptions, meetings, dinners, and other large gather-

91

A detail from the colorful panoramic painting of early California ranch days.

Statues are arranged for display at various heights on the walls of the Galeria.

ings. Instead of the paintings once displayed here, the walls now hold an eclectic assortment of sculpture arranged at various heights. The saints, angels, gargoyles, and other statues that make up this collection were gathered for this unusual display from different sections of the Inn.

One painting remains in the Galeria—a colorful panoramic oil painting which depicts a romanticized version of early California ranch days. A few stains are visible, attesting to years of hanging above the food counter in the corner drugstore that is now occupied by the Mission Inn Museum.

The large stained glass window on the end wall is opaque Tiffany glass, matching those in the St. Francis Chapel.

The carved gilt marriage altar of the St. Cecilia Chapel is dated 1740 while the altar cross of filigree brass is estimated to be older.

ST. CECILIA CHAPEL

Tucked into a corner of the St. Francis Atrio, behind an often locked door, is a tiny wedding chapel dedicated to St. Cecilia, the patron saint of music. It is one of the most restricted areas in the Mission Inn because of the age and condition of the artifacts there. The antique marriage altar of gesso and gold leaf, dated 1740, is one of the oldest objects at the Inn. Above the altar, the carved wooden ceil-

The plain wooden doors of the St. Cecilia Chapel were replaced with carved, hand-finished doors in 1996.

ing panel, shining with gold leaf, depicts God holding a crucifix and surrounded by angels. The chapel's single window, entitled *Monk at the Organ,* is signed by Louis Comfort Tiffany and portrays a monk in a rich brown robe with his hands on the keyboard of an old style organ.

Prior to the construction of the St. Francis Chapel, the St. Cecilia Chapel was the only wedding chapel in the hotel. Originally located at the back of the stage

The St. Cecilia Wedding Chapel or Oratory as it appeared before it was moved from the stage of the Cloister Music Room in 1957.

of the Cloister Music Room, the St. Cecilia Chapel was moved to its present site in 1957. This chapel reflects the Miller family's interest in music as does the Cloister Music Room's memorial window featuring Frank Miller's first wife, Isabella Hardenburg Miller, as St. Cecilia. Although the move separated the chapel from the memorial window, both remain tributes to Isabella Miller's love of music and her many personal contributions to the early development of the hotel.

In 1996 the Friends of the Mission Inn funded the restoration and cleaning of the priceless artifacts in the St. Cecilia Chapel. Among the selected items were the antique marriage altar, sacrament chest, the crucifix on a pedestal, the ceiling panel and cherub, the ceiling crucifix, and three torchieres. Richard Salas, a gilder of great repute, did the gilding work, taking almost three months to complete the painstaking work of repair, re-carving, and re-applying gold leaf on some of these delicate pieces.

The ceiling has a most unusual carved center piece, a representation of God, supporting Christ the Son on a Tau-shaped or Egyptian cross.

Signed by Louis C. Tiffany, the MONK AT THE ORGAN is made of Favril glass, a process developed by the noted glass artist.

94

UPPER FLOORS

"While music is wonderful and painting appeals to us greatly, architecture lives on forever."

— Frank Miller

Overlooking the enclosed patio on the north is Authors Row, with the arched openings, grilled gates and windows of the Alhambra Suite on the east.

Small balconies, patios, turrets, towers, arches and domes form the fascinating and myriad architectural delights of the upper floors of the Mission Inn.

ALHAMBRA COURT

A trip to the upper floors is rewarded with a magnificent view overlooking the Court of the Birds. The water of the pool shimmers through the tops of palms; walkways meander through the garden; and a variety of arches, turrets, and peaked rooftops punctuate the sky.

Passing from the hallway of the Mission Wing to the Cloister Wing on the third floor, the corridor approaches a narrow set of stairs illuminated by several large stained glass windows, the most prominent of which depicts Christ as the Good Shepherd. A landing on the stairway leads to one entrance, through a low door, to what has traditionally been called Aunt Alice's Suite. Aunt Alice refers to Alice Miller Richardson, Frank Miller's sister, who managed the Mission Inn for over fifty years and resided in this suite from around 1924 until her death in 1937. Her room is more formally known as *La Posada de los Astros,* or Star Lodge, as Alice was an amateur astronomer.

The stairs wind upward to a dim passage that opens into the Alhambra Court, named after the great Moorish Palace in Granada, Spain. Prior to

The Carmel dome, patterned after the Carmel Mission, originally contained a telescope where star gazers could observe the heavens through round portholes.

Christ the Good Shepherd.

A view through an archway reveals the Alhambra roof-garden and the Carmel dome.

The Alhambra balcony over-looking the Spanish Patio.

The Alhambra Suite.

Richard and Patricia Nixon stand before the distinctive carved mantle of the fireplace in the Alhambra Suite.

The colorful Alhambra Court is a secluded area on the top floor of the Cloister Wing.

Surmounting the Ramona Dome is a lantern of cathedral artglass panels. Each contains scenes or characters from Helen Hunt Jackson's novel, "Ramona."

The sun sets behind the carillon at the end of "a perfect day."

the room additions on this level in the early 1920s, this courtyard area was used for roller skating and tennis. One of the largest suites at the Inn, the Alhambra Suite, opens onto the Court. It features a bedroom and a large living room with beam ceilings, curved windows, and a massive fireplace with a deeply carved mantel. Doors in the Suite, opposite the courtyard, open on to a narrow balcony and an exotic view of the Inn's skyline framed by Moorish arches.

Stunning views both day and night.

Authors Row was named in honor of writers who were frequent guests at the hotel.

A glimpse of the Amistad Dome from Authors Row.

AUTHORS ROW TO AMISTAD DOME

On the north side of the Alhambra Court another short flight of stairs leads to Authors Row. The first of these rooms was built in 1923 as the private suite of Frank Miller and his second wife, Marion Clark Miller. Additional hollow-tile rooms were added in 1928, each named in honor of a writer such as Zona Gale (Frank Miller's biographer) and songwriter Carrie Jacobs Bond, who frequented the Inn in the early part of the twentieth century.

Beyond Authors Row is an overlook of the St. Francis Atrio and the rooms located above the St. Francis Chapel and the Galeria. These rooms are part of the last wing added to the hotel—the International Rotunda Wing—built between 1929 and 1931. The most stunning of these is the Anne Cameron Suite, initially named in honor of a local teacher and short-story writer, and now better known as the Bridal Suite. The room occupies the space below the tiled Amistad Dome, and

the curved ceiling of this suite is actually the interior of the dome. The patio outside the Anne Cameron Suite offers a spectacular view down the Rotunda's spiral stairway.

In the Suite stands a tall double-storied fireplace. Smiling down on guests from the fireplace mantle is the *Portrait of Madame Korevo*, a detailed and skillful study of the Countess Katherine Korevo, a lady of the Russian Court. This oil portrait is dated 1900 and signed by Russian artist Ilia Repin, who was

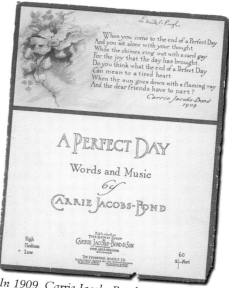

In 1909, Carrie Jacobs Bond wrote "A Perfect Day" at the Mission Inn.

The Amistad Dome can be seen beyond a row of hotel rooms facing the small Garden of the Sky patio.

The room named after songwriter Carrie Jacobs Bond on Authors Row.

considered the best portrait painter in Russia at the turn of the century. In 1904 the painting was sent by the artist to be exhibited at the St. Louis World's Fair, after which it disappeared along with several other Russian paintings from that exhibit. Years later the portrait appeared in a private art collection in San Francisco. Frank Miller purchased *Madame Korevo* at a public auction, and it has been at the Mission Inn ever since.

The Amistad Dome covers a large 20-foot square room known as the Bridal Suite.

Alhambra Court as viewed from Authors Row.

The PORTRAIT OF MADAME KOREVO, signed and dated 1900, by noted Russian portrait artist Ilia Repin.

The International Rotunda

In designing the International Rotunda, Peter Weber of the architectural firm of G. Stanley Wilson, drew upon a number of European models. From the top of the spiral stairway, the Rotunda is a whirlpool of pillars, arches, and wrought iron, swirling downwards six floors to a small fountain at the basement level. A statue of a peasant with two geese under his arms stands in the middle of the fountain, a replica of the "Gooseman Fountain" in Nuremberg, Germany.

The circle of arches and supporting pillars on each floor is made of concrete which was poured into wooden forms. The imprint of each board with its own special grain pattern shows clearly in the decades-old cement. The offices behind the arches are lined with oak and decorative leaded-glass windows.

At the bottom of the Rotunda stands a replica of the Gooseman Fountain of Nuremberg, Germany.

Inset into the arches are 55 ceramic-tile plaques, most representing symbols of nations around the world. The Mexican eagle with the snake in its mouth follows the black eagle of Charles V of Spain and the chrysanthemum of Japan. Frank Miller installed these plaques in the International Rotunda to emphasize his passion and concern for world affairs. Prior to 1917 he worked diligently to keep the United States out of the war raging in Europe. He founded the Riverside Peace Society, which became important enough to attract the financial support of steel magnate Andrew Carnegie. Miller later added a plaque with Carnegie's name to the national symbols in the Rotunda.

The Andrew Carnegie plaque.

In spite of this strong belief in peace, Miller pitched in wholeheartedly in many ways to support the war effort once American troops went to France. He accepted membership on the prestigious National War Work Council which included such prominent Americans as William Howard Taft, Henry Ford, and John D. Rockefeller, all former visitors to the Inn.

After the war, Miller continued his efforts for peaceful international understanding. He hosted many times the Institute of International Relations, the first

The wrought iron initials are those of Juan Bautista de Anza, the Spanish explorer.

Looking upwards from the ground floor of the International Rotunda.

A view of the upper and lower levels of the Oriental Court from the Rotunda with the carillon in the background.

such organization in the West, which he co-founded with USC President Rufus B. Von Kleinsmid. Along with Stanford President Ray Lyman Wilbur, a Riverside Poly High School graduate, and other scholars, they promoted the relatively new study of international relations. John F. Kennedy attended an Institute conference at the Inn in 1940, while attending a summer session at Stanford.

Even though he had developed an intense interest in modern world affairs, Miller remained fascinated with the past, particularly that of California and the missions. As always, this passion was reflected in his building projects. In the wrought iron railings at the top of the Rotunda, he placed the initials of California's 21 missions. The lower railings feature the initials of the presidents of the missions, the easiest to identify being PJS, Padre Junipero Serra. Included with the padres are a few secular Spanish explorers who reached California, such as JB de A, Juan Bautista de Anza. Through it all are bells and crosses, the ultimate symbols of the missions.

The circular stairs of the International Rotunda spiral downward six floors.

MISSION INN MUSEUM

In 1976, four decades after Frank Miller's death, the City of Riverside purchased the Mission Inn. The Riverside City Council established the Mission Inn Foundation, a non-profit organization, with a volunteer board of directors to oversee operations and manage the property. Public ownership of the hotel lasted over eight years and ended with the sale to a developer in 1985. The Foundation's purpose then shifted from daily operations to preserving the historical and architectural integrity of the Mission Inn through education and the exhibition, interpretation, and care of the art and artifact collections.

Arts and Crafts style suite made expressly for the Mission Inn, featuring the Rain Cross housemark.

The Millers' bell collection numbered almost 800 bells, representing many countries and many cultures.

Chinese warrior,
made of clay
and lacquer in
the nineteenth
century.

A challenging phase of planning and developing a museum within the Inn began. Funded by a National Endowment for the Humanities grant and generous community support, the Foundation staff and consultants worked on plans for the museum during the years the Inn was closed for restoration.

In 1992, after the Inn was sold to Duane R. Roberts, the current location at the corner of Mission Inn Avenue and the Riverside Mall was selected. Talented craftsmen transformed the old drugstore that previously occupied the corner into the Mission Inn Museum which opened in May 1993.

Operated by the Mission Inn Foundation and staffed by volunteers, the Museum is open seven days a week and uses the collections to tell the story of the Inn and the Miller family. The Museum also provides changing exhibits, educational programs, and curatorial care of the collections. Children particularly enjoy the barber shop exhibit and the intriguing Asian collection. Long-term exhibits include three Papal Court wax figures from the Catacomb exhibits, reminders of the eclectic objects once displayed there. Other treasures include hundreds of bells, crosses, paintings, sculpture, Arts and Crafts furnishings and oddities which reflect the world vision and tastes of Frank Miller. A variety of temporary exhibit themes have ranged from water development for the newly formed colony of Riverside in the 1870s to Miller family photographs.

The spirit of Frank Miller, prominent in the city's early years, remains at the Inn among its beautiful collections, restful spaces, and rambling architecture. Daily tours of the hotel, led by the Foundation's well-informed volunteer docents, offer guests an enjoyable glimpse into the past. Brochures, pamphlets, and books

Known as a HU, this nineteenth century cast bronze wine storage vessel, is a copy of one used as early as two hundred B. C.

A gilt and lacquer figure known as a Bodhisattva sits on a lion, which is considered the vehicle of wisdom.

113

A five-storied pagoda made of lacquered wood is a copy of the famous one in Nikko, Japan.

Detail of pagoda.

Henry Chapman Ford's California mission paintings and a handsome statue of a Franciscan padre reflect the Mission Revival movement's interest in California's Spanish heritage.

written and published by Foundation staff document an important era in the history of Southern California.

In a unique partnership with the privately owned hotel, the non-profit Mission Inn Foundation continues to preserve and promote Frank Miller's dream of creating the romantic ambiance of the early California missions in Riverside.

RESTORATION AND RENEWAL

After Frank Miller's death in 1935, his daughter Allis and son-in-law DeWitt Hutchings carried on his tradition of warm hospitality. But times were hard. No longer did Easterners and their entourages spend entire winters in Southern California. Business recovered some during World War II as young officers and cadets from March Field and other nearby military bases filled the rooms and jitterbugged in the Lea Lea Room. Still the Inn deteriorated.

In the early 1950s both Allis and DeWitt died, leaving the property to their three children. This third generation, who had grown up running through the corridors of the Inn and hiding in its Catacombs, sold the hotel in 1956 to San Francisco hotel magnate Ben Swig, owner of the famous Fairmont Hotel.

Termite extermination preparatory to the commencement of restoration.

Scaffolding surrounded the Mission Wing. Unreinforced brick in these exterior walls was ultimately replaced with conventional frame construction for earthquake safety.

Swig's purchase introduced a 20-year era of Inn sales, repossessions, bankruptcies, and unfortunate attempts to modernize. Throughout this troubled time, the Inn retained its aura of magnificence, a grand old dowager, tattered at the edges, but still in demand for major events and celebrations.

Finally the city of Riverside stepped in to protect this important community asset. Through the Riverside Redevelopment Agency, the Inn was purchased in 1976, ushering in public ownership and the beginnings of restoration. Money was raised through grants and campaigns. Volunteers worked on projects, and organizations such as the Junior League restored individual hotel rooms.

Progress was made, but the city had to provide some operating funds, a decision that was politically unpopular in some quarters. After much public debate, the Redevelopment Agency sold the Inn to a private developer, the Carley Capital Group, for $3 million. In June 1985, for the first time in 107 years, the doors of the Mission Inn closed.

The new owners immediately surveyed the property to identify a wide variety of structural and mechanical deficiencies requiring correction.

At upper left, note the slanted underside of the old stairway from the hotel lobby to the guest rooms above. This stairway was removed and its replacement more gracefully sweeps behind the registration desk.

They projected it would cost $30 million to renovate the Inn and require two years to complete.

The most extensive corrections were required in the hotel's oldest portion, the un-reinforced brick Mission Wing. Exterior walls were reinforced to meet current seismic codes, and sagging ceiling beams were strengthened with steel plates. Along Main Street, where the building was inadequately connected to its foundation, the original cast-iron columns were replaced with steel I-beams and anchored into reinforced concrete.

Central air-conditioning and heating took the place of unsightly and inefficient window air-conditioners. Exterior fire escapes were removed and interior fire stairs constructed.

In the newer wings, improvements were also necessary. The eastern wall of the Cloister Wing was strengthened and, in the Spanish addition and the Rotunda Wing, walls were reinforced against earthquakes. Heavy concrete ornaments, along and near Authors Row on the fourth floor, were supplanted with lightweight replicas.

The Lea Lea Room was demolished, and the Court of the Orient was restored. New plumbing was installed throughout the Inn.

Sometimes repair was not practical. The *cam-*

panario had to be replaced as did the Seventh Street arches. Both were copied to the last detail, using modern construction materials. Full replication of the reinforced concrete tree pergola around the Court of the Birds proved to be beyond budget and—except for one short duplicated section—was replaced by a simple redwood structure.

The complexity of the renovation work pushed the project $10 million over budget and six months behind schedule. On December 2, 1988 the Carley Group's cash and credit were exhausted, and all work ceased. Later that month, ownership of the Inn was transferred to Carley's principal creditor, Chemical Bank of New York.

On December 1, 1992, after four years of reporting tangled legal claims and endless restoration work, Riverside's *The Press-Enterprise* carried the headline, "Potential Inn Buyer Emerges." The

A steel horizontal truss was installed beneath the finished floor of this first floor Mission Wing hallway. Its job, in event of a strong earthquake, is to prevent the building from tearing apart at an otherwise structurally vulnerable point.

new suitor was Duane R. Roberts, chairman and chief executive officer of Entrepreneurial Capital Corporation, a Riverside-based financial and management services company.

Duane Roberts was quoted in *The Press-*

The wooden framing of the original "campanario" was severely damaged by termites and dry-rot. It has been rebuilt, atop the original brick piers, utilizing a steel frame and aluminum lath.

Enterprise as saying that the Mission Inn was "like family." Indeed the then 56-year-old Roberts, a Riverside resident for more than 40 years, spent memorable hours as a teenager exploring the old hotel. His father, Harry Roberts, in 1950 founded Butcher Boy Food Products Inc., a local meat company that became a major supplier for hamburger patties to the original McDonald's restaurant.

When young Roberts was 19, he began experimenting in the kitchen, developing what became the first commercially available frozen burrito. By the 1970s Butcher Boy was the nation's largest manufacturer of burritos and a major Riverside employer.

After selling the company in 1980, Duane Roberts formed the privately-held Entrepreneurial Capital Corp-

The Spanish Art Gallery during restoration.

oration, which is involved in real estate development and investment, merchant banking, and other financial ventures. By the time he made his bid for the Mission Inn, Roberts was a home-town success. He moved quickly and escrow closed in less than a month.

On December 24, 1992, Roberts signed all necessary papers, and the property was officially transferred to his new company: Historic Mission Inn Corporation. Riverside Inn lovers received the best present of all with the Christmas Day headline, "Roberts Closes Escrow on Mission Inn." Six days later on December 30, 1992, Duane Roberts reopened the Mission Inn with a 6:15 a.m. ribbon-cutting.

A new era for the Mission Inn had begun.

THE MISSION INN

DONE BY
ARTHUR BURNETT BENTON
THE SKETCHES BY
WM ALEXANDER SHARP
COPYRIGHTED 1907 BY A.B.BENTON

Through The Years With The Mission Inn

1870	Town of Riverside founded.
1874	Christopher Columbus Miller commissioned to expand canal system.
1875	Miller receives one city block of land in lieu of $325 for work.
	Miller family completes two-story, 12-room house on property and names it The Glenwood. In November Albert S. White is the first paying guest.
1880	Glenwood Hotel purchased for $5000 by Frank A. Miller, older son of C. C. Miller.
	Frank Miller marries Isabella Hardenburg.
1881	Congressman William McKinley visits Glenwood.
1882	Two-story addition attached to original adobe brick house.
	Allis Miller born.
1886	Seventy-five room Glenwood Hotel for sale. No buyers.
1888	John D. Rockefeller visits Glenwood Hotel.
1890	Loring Opera House completed and performers stay at Glenwood.
1897	Glenwood remodeled again.
1902	Construction begins on new Mission Revival style hotel.
	Architect: Arthur B. Benton
1903	New Glenwood Mission Inn opens with over 200 rooms.
	President Theodore Roosevelt spends night at Inn. Next morning, May 8th, the President transplants a parent navel orange tree.
1907	John Muir, naturalist, visits Inn.
1908	Seventh Street arches span entrance.
	Indian Rain Cross patented as hotel symbol.
	Isabella Hardenburg Miller dies.
1909	President William Howard Taft attends banquet and occupies chair built to hold his 335 pounds.
	Allis Miller marries DeWitt Hutchings.
1910	Andrew Carnegie at Inn for short visit.
	Frank Miller marries Marion Clark.
1910-11	Cloister Wing built encompassing Music Room, Curio Shop, offices and 45 new hotel rooms.
	Architect: Arthur B. Benton.
1911	First Western Peace Conference held at Mission Inn.
1913	Sarah Bernhardt, famous French actress, spends night.
	Henry Ford visits Mission Inn.
1913-15	Spanish Wing addition including Spanish Art Gallery,
	Spanish Patio and dining room, ten hotel rooms.
	Architect: Myron Hunt.
1914	Booker T. Washington lectures in Music Room.
	Nanking Bell from Chinese temple arrives at Inn.
1917	Cloister Walk beneath Music Room (later called the Catacombs) houses wax Pontifical Court figures and fine art.
1918	Painting *California Alps* by William Keith arrives at Inn.
1921	Mission Inn Annex built across Sixth Street to house employees.
	Expanded 1926.
1922	Secretary of Commerce, Herbert Hoover, has breakfast at Inn.
	Frank Miller co-founds the Institute of World Affairs.

1923-24	Construction of Frank Miller's apartment and Alhambra Suite on fourth floor near Carmel Tower Dome.
1926	Sweden's Crown Prince Gustavus and Princess Louise attend banquet in their honor.
	Foot bridge constructed over Sixth Street from Annex to hotel.
1928	Addition of five hotel suites above Spanish Art Gallery, each named for Miller's favorite authors. Architect: G. Stanley Wilson
1929-31	Construction of International Rotunda, Atrio with Galeria. St. Francis Chapel, Bacchus Fountain. Architect: G. Stanley Wilson.
1934	Fliers Wall established in Atrio.
	Japan's Prince and Princess Kaya visit Inn.
1935	Frank A. Miller, Master of the Inn, dies.
1936	First liquor license issued to Inn.
1939	Lea Lea Room opens.
1940	Richard Nixon and Patricia Ryan married June 21 in Presidential Suite.
	John F. Kennedy, graduate student, attends Institute of World Affairs held at Inn.
1940-45	Servicemen from nearby military camps gather at Inn.
1943	Fire damages Carillon Tower which is rebuilt later.
1947-48	Original Miller house, the Old Adobe, demolished. Site used for new swimming pool.
1951	Mission Inn's 75th Anniversary celebration.
1952	Nancy and Ronald Reagan spend wedding night at Inn.
1952-53	Allis and DeWitt Hutchings die leaving majority interest in hotel to their children.
1955-56	Heirs sell hotel to Benjamin Swig of San Francisco, who renovates and modernizes hotel.
1957	Presidential Suite converted to cocktail lounge.
	Public auction of excess hotel furniture and artwork.
1961	Mission Inn designated California Historical Landmark Number 761.
1966	Riverside's Main Street converted to pedestrian mall.
1967-69	Inn sold to Goldco and MII Corporation.
1969	Mission Inn named Riverside City Landmark Number 1.
	Friends of the Mission Inn, a volunteer support group, founded by Patsy O'Toole.
	Three hundred UC Riverside students housed in Mission Inn.
1970	Glenwood Tavern opens in Cloister Wing with English pub atmosphere.
	Inn reverts to Benjamin Swig, mortgage holder.
1971	Inn purchased by Urban Housing Company of Los Angeles.
	Mission Wing converted into 137 apartments.
1976	Connecticut General Life Insurance Company acquires hotel at foreclosure sale for $2.4 million.
	Mission Inn 100th Anniversary celebrated November 22.
	Riverside Redevelopment Agency buys Inn. Mission Inn Foundation organized to manage hotel—Arthur Littleworth, first president.
1977	Mission Inn designated a National Historic Landmark, first in Riverside County.
1985	Carley Capital Group buys Inn and begins an estimated two-year restoration.
1988-89	Chemical Bank forecloses on Carley Capital Group.
1990	Mission Inn once again for sale.
1992	Inn sold December 24 to Riverside businessman Duane R. Roberts—opens six days later.
1993	Mission Inn Foundation opens Museum on the Mall. Friends of the Mission Inn relocates Inn-Credible Gift Corner.
	Mission Inn Grand Opening Gala.
	Duane Roberts initiates first annual Christmas Festival of Lights.
1995	Section of Seventh Street renamed Mission Inn Avenue.
1998	Former President Gerald Ford visits Inn.

ACKNOWLEDGEMENTS

The Friends of the Mission Inn, a non-profit organization, published this book with funds primarily derived from sales at the Inn-Credible Gift Corner. Located in the Mission Inn on the Mall, the gift shop is staffed by dedicated volunteers seven days a week and expertly managed by Nadine Hausladen. Since 1969, the Friends of the Mission Inn have invested hundreds of thousands of dollars in the restoration and purchase of art, artifacts, furniture and room renovation at the historic Mission Inn.

The Friends extend sincere appreciation to Duane R. Roberts, owner of the Mission Inn who allowed photographers and writers access to the building during the preparation of this book. Our deepest gratitude to Ted Weggeland of the Entrepreneurial Hospitality Corporation for his special assistance and to Dorie Vermilyn who helped in ways too numerous to count. We are also most grateful to Robert Routh in Marketing and hotel staff Gale Snow, Mary Truesdale and Chef Gary Palm for their assistance. A special thanks to Engineer Steve Huffman and engineering staff Tony Asis, Terry McKiernan, Dennis Cosencino and Willie Valez who made it possible to take photos in the busy hotel.

The Publication Committee, most ably chaired by Elaine Ford, consisted of a group of volunteer writers, photographers and contributors who combined their abilities in a team effort. Under the editorial guidance of Barbara Moore, independent talents were blended together to tell the story of the Mission Inn. Text material was researched, written and contributed by Allene Archibald (Mission Inn Foundation) Alan Curl (Riverside Municipal Museum), Joan Hall, Kevin Hallaran, Philippa Jones, Walter Parks, Michael Rounds and Juanita Thinnes. A variety of photographs featuring the art and artifacts, impressive rooms, and captivating views of the Mission Inn were contributed by photographers Michael J. Elderman, Bob Fitch, Judith Giberson, Bill Roth, Bob Torrez, Cean Orrett of Cean One Photography Studios and John Kleinman and his assistants Cherie Hansen and Gail Johnson McMillan.

Our thanks also to Mission Inn Foundation Museum Curator of Education Nancy Wenzel and staff members Randi Brewer and Lynn Brocklebank for their valuable assistance and the use of museum photographs. Dr. Vincent Moses, Curator of History at the Riverside Municipal Museum, was most helpful in obtaining old photographs. Gladys Murphy of the University of California, Riverside, Rivera Library Special Collections, helped locate and identify early historic photographs for our use. Jackie Chamberlain of *The Press-Enterprise* deserves special recognition and gratitude for help with the newspaper's photographic archives.

While assembling the book, many individuals offered photographs, memorabilia and/or their talents, for which the Friends of the Mission Inn are most grateful. Community supporters R. A. Haight, Frances Endeman, and Carolyn Sharp shared personally owned historic photographs and postcards. Special thanks to Fred Bauman for his excellent photograph of the "tented" Mission Inn and to Dominic Budicin of Photos Unlimited and Rich Biber of FPC Graphics for technical advice and encouragement. Ken Krivanek, Betty Parks and Barbara Dooley volunteered their time for proofreading.

Our utmost gratitude to Deb Lorenzi and the RB Graphics staff for their guidance and encouragement in the development of this book, especially to designer Jennifer Disbrow, whose talents have captured and enhanced Riverside's greatest treasure...the Mission Inn.

The 1998 Board of Directors of the Friends of the Mission Inn

PHOTO CREDITS

57	Bob Fitch
58	Bob Fitch
59	Top: Bob Torrez, Historic Mission Inn
	Bottom Left: John Kleinman
	Bottom Right: Friends of the Mission Inn Collection
60	Top: Friends of the Mission Inn Collection
	Bottom: Caroline Sharp Collection
61	All Photos: Scott Haskins
62	Top & Botton: Friends of the Mission Inn Collection
63	Top & Bottom: TK Jones
64	Top Left & Right: Bill Rose
	Bottom: Michael J. Elderman
65	Top & Bottom: Mission Inn Foundation and Museum Collection
66, 67	Bob Fitch
68	Top: Historic Mission Inn
	Bottom: Friends of the Mission Inn Collection
69	Left: Scott Haskins
	Right: Bill Rose
70	Bottom Left: Dick Tullis
	Bottom Right: Bob Torrez
71	John Kleinman
72	Top Left: Judith Giberson
	Top Right: Michael J. Elderman
	Center Right: Bill Roth
	Bottom: Michael J. Elderman
73	Top: Mission Inn Foundation and Museum Collection
	Bottom: Nick Souza, *The Press-Enterprise*
74	Top: Special Collections, UCR Rivera Library
	Bottom: Michael J. Elderman
75	Dave Bauman, *The Press-Enterprise*
76, 77	Michael J. Elderman
78	Top: Michael J. Elderman
	Bottom: Friends of the Mission Inn Collection
79	Top: Robert Reed
	Left and Right: Special Collections, UCR Rivera Library
80	Top Left: Bill Roth
	Top Right: Michael J. Elderman
	Bottom: Special Collections, UCR Rivera Library
81	John Guin
82	John Guin
83	Top: Bob Torrez
	Bottom Left: Bill Rose
	Bottom Right: Bill Roth
84	Michael J. Elderman
85	Top: Historic Mission Inn
	Bottom: Bill Roth
86	Mission Inn Foundation and Museum Collection
87	Left: *The Press-Enterprise*
	Right: Bob Fitch
88	*The Press-Enterprise*
89	Top: Bill Rose
	Bottom: *The Press-Enterprise*
90	Center: Michael J. Elderman
	Bottom: Mission Inn Foundation and Museum Collection
91	Top: Bob Torrez, Historic Mission Inn
	Bottom: Caroline Sharp Collection
92	Top: Mission Inn Foundation and Museum Collection
	Bottom: Bob Torrez, Historic Mission Inn
93	All Photos: Bob Fitch
94	Top: Friends of the Mission Inn Collection
	Bottom: Bob Fitch
95	Bill Rose
96, 97	Michael J. Elderman
98	Top Left: Bob Torrez, Historic Mission Inn
	Center: Cean Orrett
	Top Right: Michael J. Elderman
99	Top: Dennis McFarland
	Bottom Left: Michael J. Elderman
	Bottom Right: Bill Rose
100	Top Left: Michael J. Elderman
	Center Left: Bob Torrez, Historic Mission Inn
	Center Right: Mission Inn Foundation and Museum Collection
	Bottom: Bob Torrez, Historic Mission Inn
101	All Photos: Michael J. Elderman
102	Top: Bob Torrez, Historic Mission Inn
	Bottom: Michael J. Elderman
103	Top Left: Michael J. Elderman
	Top Right: Bob Torrez
	Bottom: Bob Fitch
104	Michael J. Elderman
105	Top: Bob Fitch
	Left Bottom: Bob Fitch
	Right Bottom: *The Press-Enterprise*
106	Scott Haskins
107	Top: Judith Giberson
	Center and Bottom: Bob Fitch
108	John Kleinman
109	Left: Historic Mission Inn
	Right: Michael J. Elderman
110-115	All Photos: Michael J. Elderman
116, 117	Fred Bauman
118	Bob Fitch
119	Top: Steve Huffman
	Bottom: Alan Curl
120	Top: Alan Curl
	Center: *The Press-Enterprise*
121	William A. Sharp

Third End Paper: R. A. Haight

Fourth End Paper: Friends of the Mission Inn Collection

INDEX

Adobe, Old, 15, 30, 45
Alhambra Court, Suite, 97-100
Allis Miller, Daughter Of The Inn, 50, 53
Amistad Dome, 26-7, 103
Annex, 24
Anton Clock, 55-7, 70, 72
A Perfect Day, 56, 103
Arch Beach, 39. 48
Arches on Seventh Street, 21, 119
Arnold, General Henry (Hap), 79
Arts and Crafts, 68, 113
Atrio. *See* St. Francis
Aunt Alice. *See* Richardson
Authors Row, 24, 97, 103, 119

Bacchus Fountain. *See* Fountains
Barber Shop, 113
Barcelona, Spain, 55
Bells, 39
    oldest, 2, 70
    Nanking, 29, 32
Benton, Arthur B., 15, 18-19, 23, 44, 78
Bond, Carrie Jacobs, 56, 103, 105
Bodhisattva, 113
Botticelli, 60
Boxer Rebellion, 32
Bridal Suite, 103, 105
Bridge over Sixth Street, 24, 26
British Museum, 70
Brown, Bonnie, 43
Buddha, Amitabha, 74-5
Burroughs, John, 15
Butcher Boy Food Products, 120
Buttresses, 23-4, 26-7

California Alps, 36-7, 39, 48, 68, 91
California
    Dining Room, 48
    Lounge, 48
    Missions. *See* Missions
Cameron, Anne, 103
Campanario, 28-30, 45, 119-20
Cannons, 31
Carillon, 35, 56, 101
Carley Capital Group, 118-19
Carmel Tower Dome, 22
Carnegie, Andrew, 107
Carpet in lobby, 38, 40
Catacombs, 9, 46-7, 113, 117
Chapels. *See* Saints

St. Cecilia, 79, 93-4
    St. Francis, 62-3, 77, 80, 84-5, 90-3
Chemical Bank, 119
Chicago Institute of Art, 50
Chinese Warrior, 112
Christ In The Temple, 83
Christ The Good Shepherd, 98-9
Citrus, 11, 12
Cloister Music Room, 44-5, 94
Cloister Wing, 18-9, 23-4, 45-6, 119
Coats of Arms, 35
College of San Fernando, Mexico, 78
Congregational Church, 85
Cordova, Spain, 55
Court of the Birds, 23, 29, 30, 32-3, 42, 98, 119
Court of the Orient, 73, 119
Cummings, Robert, 79
Cunningham, Randy "Duke", 79

Davis, Bette, 90
De Anza, Juan Bautista, 55, 72, 107, 109
DeFore, Don, 79
Della Robbia, 72, 79-81,
Department of Agriculture, 12, 35
Disi, A.G., 72
Doolittle, Jimmy, 79
Dragons, 74
Drake, Charles, 79
Duane's Prime Steaks, 49-50, 91

Earhart, Amelia, 79
Eastern Airlines, 79
Echave, Baltazar de, 88
Entrepreneurial Capital Corporation, 119-20
Escutcheon, 1, 39

Fairmont Hotel, 117
Fliers' Wall, 78-9
Flight Into Egypt, 61
Flying Cross. See St. Francis
Ford, Henry, 107
Ford, Henry Chapman, 63-5, 115
Foss, Joe, 79
Fountains, 56
    Bacchus, 77, 84
    Gooseman, 107
Franciscan Order, 15, 45-6, 78, 82
Frank Miller Executive Dining Room, 50, 52, 54

Frank Miller, Master Of The Inn, 50
Frank Miller Suite, 103
Frank Miller Window, 82-3
Fray Junipero Serra and Don Gaspar De Portola at Monterey Bay, 67, 69
Fray Junipero Serra Meeting With The California Indians, 69
Fray Junipero Serra Praying For The Return of The Relief Ship, 69
Friends of the Mission Inn, 7, 8, 27, 63, 67, 94

Galeria, 79, 90-2
Gale, Zona, 103
Garden of the Bells, 70
Garden of the Sky, 105
Garland, Judy, 54
Gargoyles, 55-6, 92
Gazebo, 32-3
Glenn, John, 80
Glenwood Hotel, 15
    Cottages, 13
Goodhue, Harry Eldridge, 45
Gooseman Fountain. *See* Fountains,
Granada, Spain, 60, 98
Guanajuato, Mexico, 87

Haight, Albert, 62
Hall of the Gods, 73
Harrison, Benjamin, 43
Historic Mission Inn Corporation, 102
Ho-O-Kan Room, 73-4
Hu, 113
Huntington, Henry E., 14
Hunt, Myron, 18, 23, 54, 60
Hutchings, Allis Miller, 15, 54, 73, 79, 85
Hutchings, DeWitt, 73, 79, 85, 117

I Love You Truly, 56
Indian artifacts, 46
Inn-Credible Gift Corner, 7, 27
Institute of World Affairs, 107, 109
International Rotunda, 18-19, 26-7, 62, 82, 103, 107-9, 119
International Shrine to Aviators, 85

Joseph, the macaw 29-30, 45, 48-9
Junior League of Riverside, 118

Keith, William, 37, 39, 68, 91
Kennedy, John F., 109

Kilgen organ, 45-6
Korevo, Countess Katherine, 103, 105-6
Kosscheloff, Professor N. A., 60

La Posada de los Astros – Star Lodge, 98
Lea Lea Room, 73-4, 117, 119
Lobby, 39, 41, 43

McBurney, James E., 67-9
McDonald's Restaurant, 120
Madison Square Presbyterian Church, 89
Main Street Mall, 26-7
Mandarin's Journey, 74
Map, 18-9
March Field, 117
Marriage of Joseph and Mary, 88
Miller,
    Christopher Columbus, 12
    Frank Augusta, 10, 11, 13-17, 29,
    35, 50, 55-6, 60, 70, 113
    Isabella Hardenburg, 11, 13, 35,
    45-6, 94
    Marion Clark, 103
Mission Inn, 14-15
    Art, 60
    Avenue, 21-3, 27, 29
    Foundation, 9, 113, 115
    Museum, 27, 56, 73-4, 92, 111, 113
    Restaurant, 54
Missions, 23, 40, 54, 67-8, 109
    Carmel, 23-4, 65, 99
    San Gabriel, 24, 29, 65
    San Juan Capistrano, 21, 70
    San Luis Rey, 21
    San Miguel, 44
Mission Wing,18-9, 23-4, 27, 29-31, 43,
118-9
Monk at the Organ, 93, 95
Moore, Dudley, 40
Mt. Rubidoux, 16
Murdras, 74
Muir, John, 15, 39
Music Room. *See* Cloister Music Room

Nanking Bell. *See* Bells
Napoleon, the macaw, 29-30, 48-9
National Endowment of the Humanities,
113
National Historic Landmark, 7, 31
National War Work Council, 107
New Orleans, 12
Nikko, Japan, 114
Nixon, Richard and Patricia, 42, 100
Nuremburg, Germany, 55, 107

Orange County, 39
Orange Street, 22-3, 39, 46
Oriental Art, 73

Oriental Court, 109
O'Toole, Patsy, 7
Our Lady of Guadalupe, 78

Pagoda, 114
Papal Court, 46-7, 113
Parent Navel Orange Tree, 12, 35, 56
Pasadena, 14
Pergola, 30-2, 46, 119
Philippine Islands, 31
Piano, Steinway, 40
Portrait of Madame Korevo. See Korevo,
106
Prato, Italy, 77
Presidential Lounge, 42-4
    Suite, 42
Presidents, 43
Press-Enterprise, The, 119
Prince Gustavus, 42, 56
Princess Louise, 42, 56
Pushman, Hovsep, 50

Rain Cross, 2, 22-3
Ramona Dome, 101
Raphael, 60
Rayas Altar, 62, 85-7, 89
Redlands, 14
Repin, Ilia, 103
Reredo, 87, 89
Richardson, Alice Miller, 13, 63-4, 98
Rickenbacher, Eddie, 79
Riui, 74
River of Life, 2
Riverside, 12, 30
    Colony Association, 12
    Peace Society, 107
    Redevelopment Agency, 118
Roberts, Duane R., 8-9, 49, 63, 113, 119
Roberts, Harry, 120
Rockefeller, John D., 107
Rogers, Ginger, 31, 47
Rogers, Will, 47
Rondel, 90
Roosevelt, Theodore, 35, 42-3, 49, 50
Rough Riders, The, 50
Rubens, 60
Russell, Lillian, 67

Saint,
    Francis And The Flying Cross, 87
    Francis Atrio, 62, 76, 80, 82, 93
    Francis Doors, 48
    Francis Shrine, 32
    Joseph Arcade, 79
Saints, 46, 92
    Barbara, 80
    Catherine, 80
    Cecilia, 45-6, 64, 84

Chad, 69
Francis, 6, 39, 48, 55, 70, 78-9, 80,
82-3
Hubert, 72
Joseph, 87, 89
Martha, 63-4
Salas, Richard, 94
San Francisco Panama-Pacific
International Exposition, 31
San Juan Hill, 49-51, 91
Seismic code, 119
Serra, Junipero, 39, 55, 78, 109
Seville, Spain, 55
Sharp, William, 78
Sherry, William Grant, 90
Signature Room, 62
Sixth Street, 23
Skylight Dome, 42
Spanish,
    American War, 49-50
    Art Gallery, 23, 60, 62-4, 67-8, 87
    Dining Room, 54
    Patio, 34, 42, 54-9, 69, 71
    Wing, 18-19, 23, 26, 54, 60, 102,
119
Stag's head, 72
Steinway Company. *See* Piano
Stone, George Melville, 52-4
Swig, Benjamin, 68, 117
Swimming pool, 30, 35, 98

Taft, William Howard, 40, 42, 43
    Chair, 40-1, 107
The Beggar, 61
The Good Samaritan, 69
The Lost Chord, 69
Thorn Puller, 49
Through the Years, 122-3
Tibbets, Eliza and Luther, 12, 35
Tiffany, Louis Comfort, windows, 78, 85,
89, 90, 92-3, 95

Urna, 74
Ushnisha, 74

Van Brunt, Jesse, 63
Vereschagin, Vasilli, 49
Von Kleinsmid, Rufus B., 109

Washington, Booker T., 16
Waterfall, 32, 34
Weber, Peter, 107
Wendt, William, 39
Westminster Abbey, 45
White, Albert S., 13
White, Stanford, 89
Wilbur, Ray Lyman, 109
Wilson, G. Stanley, 18, 26, 62, 107